Eagle People Journal

Daily Inspiration
from Ghostdancer Shadley

GHOSTDANCER SHADLEY

with

SANDY CATHCART

NEEDLE ROCK
PRESS

Published by Needle Rock Press.

Needle Rock Press books may be purchased in bulk for ministry purposes. For
information, please email sandycathcart@gmail.com

Scripture quotations (unless otherwise specified) are taken from the HOLY
BIBLE: NEW INTERNATIONAL VERSION © 173, 1978, 1984 by
International Bible Society. All rights reserved.

ISBN-10: 1943500010
ISBN-13: 978-1943500017 (Needle Rock Press)

DEDICATION

To the family of Ghostdancer Shadley.
(Calvin, Buttons, Pahowatush)

CONTENTS

NOTE TO READERS

Ghostdancer once traveled to Israel with Grand Chief Lynda Prince. In doing so he discovered many similarities of the Jewish culture with his Native culture. The flute that David the shepherd boy played was the same flute Natives play. The tambourine Miriam played was none other than a hand drum. The name of Creator was YHWH, which is pronounced Yahweh. Most tribes in North America have some form of Yahweh or Yah in their atonal singing, but the meaning had been lost to most tribes. You can imagine Ghostdancer's joy in discovering that Yahweh is the Creator they had long adored!

Throughout this book you will see Creator referred to as "Creator Yahweh" and God the Father often referred to as "Our Great Chief and Captain."

Ghostdancer (Calvin) & Diana Shadley

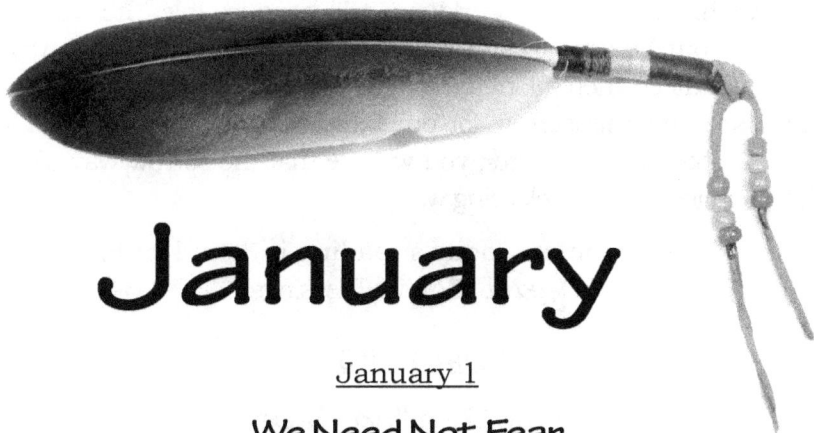

January

January 1

We Need Not Fear

Today we stand at the threshold of the unknown. A new year lies before us, yet we know not what each day will bring or which way we will choose out of the many choices. We do well to look for the blessing way—the path to a far-seeing place. It is a path that will gradually lead upward, but first it often leads through the wilderness, a place of bareness and thirst.

If we have chosen this path and chosen it well, with Creator Yahweh walking beside us, we need not fear. In Him are all the well springs that will quench our thirsty souls. His manna will strengthen us for the journey.

Choose well, warrior, for the choice brings your future.

Eagle People...Today's reading is John 4:1-13.
Pleya gi. "Go with Blessings."

January 2

Creator Yahweh Called You

Are you walking the sorrow way? Then know that Creator Yahweh walks beside you and knows you better than you know yourself. Trust your soul to his faithfulness. When he created the earth, when all the morning stars shouted for joy, he knew you, he called you by name. Knowing all the sorrow you would go

1

through, knowing all the pain, knowing every mistake you would ever make; he still called you to be his child.

He is faithful, even when we are unfaithful, because he cannot disown himself. "In this world you will have trouble," he said so himself, but he promises to walk with us along the sorrow way. He has walked there alone before us and now, though the enemy means to use this sorrow for our harm, Creator Yahweh uses it for our good. Soon, warrior, you will see that the sorrow way often intermingles with the blessing way.

Eagle People...Today's reading is John 15:1-8.
Pleya gi. "Go with Blessings."

January 3

Our Dwelling Place

A re the relentless wolves of doubt and fear howling around you? Remember, warriors, Creator Yahweh has been our dwelling place throughout all generations.

Before the mountains were born or he brought for the earth and the world, from everlasting to everlasting he alone is our Great Chief and Captain. Hide yourself in him.

Today, take time to mediate on all his works; consider the works of his hands. His works are wonderful, you know that full well. He has searched you and He knows you. He knows your coming out and your lying down. He is familiar with all your ways. At just the right time, he will silence the howl of our enemies and destroy all our foes, but remember, our foes are not flesh and blood. May we always trust in the safety of his protection.

Eagle People...Today's reading is John 15:9-17.
Pleya gi. "Go with Blessings."

January 4

The Sound of His Voice

W e have never been this way before. But Creator, Yahweh, has. This untraveled ground is unknown to us, but not to our Great Chief and Captain. He knows the dark places that steal our courage, he knows the high places that threaten to undo us, and he knows the hot stretches that rob us of breath, because he has been this way before.

It is crucial for us to never lose the sound of his voice. His voice spoke the world into existence and called us each by name, his secret name for us. His voice still speaks to our hearts when we lie on our beds at night. His thunder warns of danger, his morning song encourages us for the journey, and his night whisper helps us rest and speaks truth to our hearts.

No, we have never been this way before, but our guide is the very one who created the path. If we listen carefully, we will continue on the blessing way, even when the way is dark and sorrow crushes our souls. May we never lose the sound of Creator Yahweh's voice.

Eagle People...Today's reading is John 15:18-25.
Pleya gi. "Go with Blessings."

<u>January 5</u>

Do Not Forget

Warriors, have you forgotten the good things Creator Yahweh has done for you? If I forget Creator Yahweh, there will no more be life in these tired bones. If I forget Yahweh, my right hand will forget its skill with bow and arrow, my tongue will cleave to the roof of my mouth, my feet will nevermore dance in prayer.

Without Creator Yahweh, we have no light for the path; the way will remain dark and treacherous. Without Creator Yahweh the morning stars have no song. Without Creator Yahweh we are like a mule or horse that has no understanding but must be led with bit and bridle.

The breath of Creator Yahweh is the wind that frees us to soar on eagle wings. Pray always that we will never forget Creator Yahweh and the good things he has done for us. May we always trust in Creator Yahweh's unfailing love!

Eagle People...Today's reading is John 15:26-16:4.
Pleya gi. "Go with Blessings."

January 6

You Cannot Hide

Have you been trying to hide from Creator Yahweh's Spirit? Do you hope that he does not see the doubt and fear inside you? Has his presence become a harsh light of judgment on your soul? Do you feel you are unworthy to come into his presence?

This is a lie from the enemy, the evil trickster, the destroyer of our souls. Creator Yahweh sees inside of you. He knows every doubt, every fear. Before a word is on your tongue he knows it completely. You cannot flee from his presence. You cannot hide from his glory. If you make your bed with the evil trickster, hiding behind clouds of darkness, Creator Yahweh is there. If you rise on the wings of the morning and settle on the far side of the sea, even there Creator Yahweh's hand will hold you fast. The darkest of night cannot hide you. When you wake, he will still be with you.

No, warrior, you are not worthy, but he has chosen you and taken the judgment that should have been yours upon himself. Praise Creator Yahweh!

You are fearfully and wonderfully made. Let Creator Yahweh's presence wash you clean.

Eagle People...Today's reading is Psalm 139.
Pleya gi. "Go with Blessings."

January 7

Speak of The Good Things

It is good, warriors, to speak of the good things Creator Yahweh has done for us. Speak of them as the morning sun spills its light over you. Talk of them in your going out through the city gates and places of meeting.

Remember them when you use the skill Creator Yahweh has given you. Willingly share with all who will listen.

Creator Yahweh is close to the brokenhearted and saves those who are crushed in spirit. He hears all who cry out to him. Remember the good things he has done when you come into your house at night. Sing of them over the evening meal and write them upon the

4

tablets of your children's hearts. Speak always of the wonders of our Great Chief and Captain's love.

Eagle People...Today's reading is John 16:5-16.
Pleya gi. "Go with Blessings."

Shorter Than We First Thought

Warriors, are you discouraged and weary? Does the act of scaling the utmost height seem far out of your grasp? Consider this old man who keeps one moccasin plodding in front of the other. This journey, though now it seems impossibly long, is much shorter than we first thought.

Look for glimpses of Creator Yahweh's beauty along the way, feel his warm breath caress your face. He is still there, beside you, even when sorrows fall heavy on your shoulders and weariness crushes your heart. He is there in the unexpected places and in unexpected hours. Be still, and let his comfort encourage and strengthen you.

This trouble will pass, warrior, stand firm.

Eagle People...Today's reading is John 16:17-32.
Pleya gi. "Go with Blessings."

January 9

Dark Waters

Warriors, have you come to the waters, deep and wide, that will not let you cross? Take heart! Creator Yahweh will part the waters at the perfect time. Do not rush ahead or try to go around. This is a time of resting. Creator Yahweh will remove the obstacle when it is time for you to move again. He may part the waters so that you will walk across on dry ground. Or he may bring a companion with a boat that will carry you safely across. Or he may lift you up on eagle wings and fly you across in an instant.

The way is already known to our Great Chief and Captain. These dark waters are not a surprise to him. Rest in his unfailing love.

Eagle People...Today's reading is John 16:16-24.
Pleya gi. "Go with Blessings."

January 10

Morning Stars Sing!

In the morning let Creator Yahweh hear your voice warriors. As the morning stars sing together, wait expectantly before him. As sunlight spills over the eastern sky, bow before his presence. Lay your requests before him. Take refuge in him and he will spread his protection over you. He will surround you with favor as with a shield. Sing for joy and be glad! No matter where the path leads today, he will make it straight before you.

Do not listen to the voice of your enemies. Not one word from their mouths can be trusted. Their hearts are filled with malice and their throat is an open grave. With their tongues they lie to you. Take refuge in Creator Yahweh. He will spread his protection over you.

Yahweh. Yahweh. Yahweh. Love his name and rejoice in him!

Eagle People...Today's reading is is Psalm 5.
Pleya gi. "Go with Blessings."

January 11

Press in Close

Sometimes it is hard for this old man to keep one moccasin moving in front of the other. It is then I call out to Creator Yahweh to shed new light on his path that I may follow it to the very end. It is my heart that fails me, not in a physical sense, but in the spiritual realm. My heart deceives me and tells me I am foolish to think this old Indian will complete the task his Great Chief and Captain has given him. In times like these, I press in close to Creator Yahweh and let the words of his *Sacred Writings* encourage my heart toward the goal.

Yes. My heart is deceitful above all things. But Creator Yahweh is greater than my heart, and he knows everything! He will bring me to the land of the living, a place of incredible beauty! I close my eyes and dance now, in the spiritual realm where this tired old Indian receives strength.

Eagle People...Today's reading is Psalm 118.
Pleya gi. "Go with Blessings."

January 12

A Spacious Place

Warrior, is your back pressed hard against cold stone? Cry out to Creator Yahweh! Because he loves you, his ear is tuned to your voice. He will bring you to a spacious place, the place where antelope run and eagles soar, where rivers sing and the sweet fragrance of his breath blows across the fields. Creator Yahweh is with you. There is no reason to be afraid. What harm can mere mortals do when our Great Chief and Captain carries your soul?

Place your life in his hands, Creator Yahweh is your champion. If you continue to walk with him, there will come a day when you will look in triumph on your enemies. Every arrow will find its mark and Creator Yahweh's strength will be your defense. Shouts of joy and victory will resound in the tents of Creator Yahweh's people!

Eagle People...Today's reading is Psalm 31.
Pleya gi. "Go with Blessings."

January 13

Endless Love

Warriors, give thanks to Creator Yahweh! He is good. Everything about him is good. He opens up the gates to his village and calls out, "Come in!" All who are tired and weary, all who feel like dust beneath a thundering herd of buffalo, all whose strength has failed them. Come in! Buy without money. Drink till you are no longer thirsty. Eat the harvest of his hands.

Can you believe it? Creator Yahweh rises to show you compassion. His love is endless. It never quits. It stretches beyond the birthplace of the stars and is not hemmed in by the counting of minutes. It is a warm blanket wrapped around you at all times. Give thanks to Creator Yahweh for he is good, his love endures forever.

Eagle People...Today's reading is Psalm 33.
Pleya gi. "Go with Blessings."

January 14

Never Too Late

Warriors, have you strayed from the Faithful Way? It is never too late to return to the path Creator Yahweh has set before you. When I was young, I too, strayed off the path of Creator Yahweh's commands, and my soul became weary with sorrow. My face was pressed low in the dust until my soul was consumed with longing for my Great Chief and Captain's face.

Now I run in the path of Creator Yahweh's commands, for he has broadened my understanding and has caused me to walk his way. I meditate on his *Sacred Writings* and allow his words to strengthen and delight my innermost being.

It is never too late. Choose the Faithful Way, set your heart on Creator Yahweh's commands, hold fast to your Captain and Chief. By returning to the path of Creator Yahweh's commands, you will not be put to shame.

Eagle People...Today's reading is Psalm 34.
Pleya gi. "Go with Blessings."

January 15

Gift of Life

Warriors, are you walking the way of beauty? Thank Creator Yahweh for the courage to do so. He who set the stars in place, He who created us in his image, gives good gifts to all.

Praise him for his amazing gift of life. Praise him for all he has created. Praise him for his Holy Spirit who comforts us in our sorrow, corrects us when we are wrong and leads us in the right way.

Lift your voice in song to our Great Chief and Captain. Dance your prayers to him. Throw your thoughts toward him. Let all that has breath praise his holy name. Yahweh. Yahweh. Yahweh. The more we focus our thoughts on him, the more we will walk in beauty.

Eagle People...Today's reading is Psalm 37:1-13.
Pleya gi. "Go with Blessings."

January 16

Eagle People

Do not forget, warriors, Creator Yahweh seeks "eagle people," people who learn to walk alone with him; people who no longer depend on the continual help and faith of others. This is what I have learned from Lettie Cowman, the author of *Streams in the Desert*.

As Lettie says, "Relationship is necessary; inspiration is necessary; the wisdom of others is necessary; assistance is often necessary." We must not completely isolate ourselves from our brothers and sisters, aunties and uncles, and elders, but our souls yearn to be alone with Creator Yahweh.

We must trust him in times of isolation, even seek those times when we soar alone with him. It is in these alone times that our Great Chief and Captain does a new work within our souls and we learn to soar in loftier air. Vision quests are about being alone. They are times we set aside the regular cares of this world and seek an audience with Creator Yahweh, but eagle people need more. Eagle people dare to find times alone where they can hear his whisper in the midst of daily life.

Eagle People...Today's reading is Psalm 37:14-40.
Pleya gi. "Go with Blessings."

January 17

Soar to the Heights

Yesterday we talked about eagle people. One of the ways we can truly let our spirits soar to the heights is to be in the Sacred Writings day by day. It may be good to have a special place for this. Our grandfathers liked to get close to the earth. This old man prefers his easy chair. Once you are in your special place and before reading, settle your spirit and rest. Quiet your heart. Ask Creator Yahweh to speak to you. Then read his words.

Creator Yahweh's Word is living. It will speak truth to your heart. If you have questions, don't be afraid to ask, my wife and her friends are women and men of the Word. They will help you to better

9

understand how to apply Creator Yahweh's words to your daily life. Together, we can help each other to soar above the circumstances that try to crush our souls. Let us yearn for Creator Yahweh's words more than warm fry bread.

Eagle People...Today's reading is John 16:31-33.
Pleya gi. "Go with Blessings."

January 18

Your Mission

Warriors, we imagine in the wonder of putting our hand in Creator Yahweh's that we will be taken to the mountaintop to see far into the future. And we hear a voice saying, "Look! Look! See that distant Sacred Mountain? That is the goal of your mission. That is where every step of your way is leading."

So we head out, but instead of the mountaintop we find ourselves in the valley, shrouded and lost in darkness. And The Voice in our ear says something quite different from what we expected. Our mission, warriors, is to take one step at a time, even when we don't yet see where it all is leading or what the grand plan is, or what our overall mission in life is. Trust Creator Yahweh. He will lead us.

Eagle People...Today's reading is Hebrews 12:1-3.
Pleya gi. "Go with Blessings."

January 19

We Are His People

Creator Yahweh has always kept a remnant for himself, a small group of people who remain true to him after everyone else turns away. In the *Sacred Writings* Jacob's offspring is often pictured in this way. The prophecies also fit well with our people. There will come a day when we will no longer rely on those who struck us down but will truly rely on Creator Yahweh, the Holy One of Israel.

Our Great Chief and Captain is doing a new thing. Do you not perceive it? It springs up like streams in the desert as he cuts a path through the wasteland.

We are his people, his chosen, the people he formed for himself that we may proclaim his praise.

Apart from him there is no Savior. From ancient days he has revealed and saved and proclaimed. He is Creator Yahweh, our Holy One, our Creator, our King! He will lead us each step of the way. Whether lofty mountaintops, barren wastelands, or foggy valleys, he has gone before and left a way for us to follow. Take courage, warriors, your times are in his mighty hand.

Eagle People...Today's reading is Psalm 23.
Pleya gi. "Go with Blessings."

January 20

Day by Day

Warriors, our calling here on earth is also one that we share with every tribe and nation, but it is no less your individual calling, even though it is shared. The calling is this: to do what you can moment by moment, day by day, step by step to make the world a better place...following the leading and guidance of Creator Yahweh's Spirit within you and around you.

At some point in our lives our calling may involve some grand experience where we catch a glimpse of Creator Yahweh's face and say to ourselves, "This is my purpose in life. I know it! I know it!" But our calling is also here in the darkness and the days of small things and mundane moments.. It is here we need to bring more goodness, thankfulness, kindness, forgiveness, truth and life into the world, each day.

Eagle People...Today's reading is Romans 13:8-10.
Pleya gi. "Go with Blessings."

January 21

Ravenous Wolves

Warriors, do you feel as if the ravenous wolves of worry and doubt are surrounding you once again? Seek Creator Yahweh with all your strength, hide his Word in your heart. This poor old Indian cried and Creator Yahweh heard him. He delivered me out of all my troubles. My Great Chief and Captain helped me. He brought me out of a deep pit, one I had dug myself, and he set my feet on solid rock.

Then the wolves came and pushed me back until I was about to fall back into that pit, but once again I called out to Creator Yahweh and he helped me. Never give up calling on the Name of Creator Yahweh. He is my strength and defense. In him, I am like a young lion ready to knock out the howling wolves with one swipe. Shouts of joy and victory resound once again in the teepees of the righteous!

Eagle People…Today's reading is Romans 13:11-14.
Pleya gi. "Go with Blessings."

January 22

The Sacred Mountain

Warriors, perhaps you are wondering why this old Indian is so big on the *Sacred Writings?* It is because I lived many years loving Creator Yahweh but never quite understanding the concept of salvation. I would climb *Cheelaqsdi,* the Sacred Mountain where our people did vision quests. I would meet with Creator Yahweh, the Living God, in that place where thousands upon thousands of angels were in joyful assembly.

But then I would climb down the mountain and face the journey in my own strength. It was as if since I'm Native American, I just kept Creator Yahweh upon the Sacred Mountain, only calling for him in times of crisis. While in my babe-in-Christ mode, he covered me, but he expects us to get off milk and mature.

In my case, it took quite a few years, but finally, through reading the *Sacred Writings,* I began to grow stronger and kept Creator Yahweh with me, not just upon the Sacred Mountain, but also down in the valley where I take my day-by-day steps.

Eagle People…Today's reading is Romans 8:12-17.
Pleya gi. "Go with Blessings."

January 23

Be Strong!

Warriors, are you staring into darkness so deep that you fear to take a step forward? "Be strong!" your Great Chief and Captain calls, "Be of good courage." This is a time to grit your teeth and steady your heart, to slow it to the beat of a sleeping man. You can only do this by calling on Creator Yahweh to give you peace and to give you strength. As you stare into a wall of darkness where you must soon tread, there is no light to illuminate the path, nothing to mark the treacherous boundaries you know exist. One wrong step and all is lost. Discouragement slashes its sharp edge into your heart.

"Have I not commanded you?" Creator Yahweh's voice calls out. "Be strong!" It does not matter how weak you feel, or how foolish, your Captain and Chief has gone before; he knows the way. Listen for the echo of His voice as he leads you, not around this dark valley, but directly through it, like an arrow flying straight and true.

Eagle People...Today's reading is Joshua 1:1-6.
Pleya gi. "Go with Blessings."

January 24

Stop & Wait

Warriors, I have discovered that when thick clouds veil the sun, it's a good time to stop and wait for the blast of sunlight that will soon pour through a break in the clouds.

It is then that you will hear the echo of Creator Yahweh's voice as your fingers cling to the rock for support.

Let the hot wind of his breath fall over you and breathe courage into your soul. Close your eyes and allow the strengthening quivers to flow through muscle and tendon. With each pulse you will feel stronger, until at last you will stand as determined and full of faith as the shepherd boy, David, who was armed with nothing more than a slingshot and five small arrows. While you are waiting for this break in the storm, take time to rest, warrior, for this rest is part of his plan.

Eagle People...Today's reading is Joshua 1:7-9.
Pleya gi. "Go with Blessings."

January 25

Drumbeat of Heaven

Yesterday we talked about the need for rest. In Lettie Cowman's *Streams in the Desert,* John Ruskin talks about the music of heaven and how our lives are a part of Creator Yahweh's song. He calls it the melody of our life and explains that the music is separated here and there by rests. "During those rests," Ruskin says, "we foolishly believe we have come to the end of the song." I've learned that Creator Yahweh often forces these times of rest through sickness, disappointed plans, and frustrated efforts.

Perhaps it's because of being Native American, but I truly grieve when the drumbeat of heaven falls silent, especially when it is a sudden and unexpected pause. Yet how my heart sings when the silence is broken at just the right time by a skillful flute player. It is then I am assured that the rest is part of the making of the music. The pause sets everything in place for the next note. In times like these it is good to remember that Creator Yahweh does not write the music of our lives without a plan, and times of rest are part of that wondrous plan.

Eagle People...Today's reading is Psalm 91.
Pleya gi. "Go with Blessings."

January 26

The Speech of Heaven

Warriors, do you hear Creator Yahweh's voice upon the singing wind? The heavens declare Creator Yahweh's glory. Day after day they pour forth speech. There is no tongue or language where his voice is not heard. Creator Yahweh's voice thunders over the mighty waters; it strikes with flashes of lightning; it shakes the desert; it calms the raging sea.

Yes, there is still evil in this world, but Creator Yahweh has overcome evil. We are hard pressed on every side, but not crushed. We are struck down but not destroyed. Persecuted, but not abandoned.

The wolves may tear our bodies to pieces but they cannot touch our souls. Victory is reachable!

Our Great Chief and Captain is still writing our stories of life and loss, death and hope, and he is still in the business of turning what the enemy means for bad into something wonderful and good. Be still. Listen. Tune in to the sound of Creator Yahweh's voice.

Eagle People...Today's reading is Psalm 29.
Pleya gi. "Go with Blessings."

January 27

Walk The Spirit Way

Walk the Spirit Way, warriors, and you will not gratify the desires of the flesh. For these two are in opposition to one another. The flesh desires what is contrary to the Spirit, and the Spirit what is contrary to the flesh. Creator Yahweh does not intend that we do whatever we want. Instead, we are to listen for Creator Yahweh's voice before we take each step.

Whoever walks the Flesh Way will walk into destruction. Whoever walks the Spirit Way will walk into eternal life. Make a careful exploration of who you are and the work Creator Yahweh has given you, and then sink yourself into that. When we walk in the Spirit Way our hearts are filled with love for our Great Chief and Captain and love for others.

So then, while we have opportunity let us do good to all people and especially those who walk the Spirit Way with us. And let us not lose heart in doing good, for at just the right time we will soar with eagles!

Eagle People...Today's reading is Galatians 5:22-26.
Pleya gi. "Go with Blessings."

January 28

Sing for Joy!

Warriors, here is a good way to walk in beauty. Awake every morning fully aware of Creator Yahweh's unfailing love. Close your eyes in sleep with his sweet name trembling from your lips. Walk all your paths placing your feet in his steps. Sing for joy and be glad all your days.

Creator Yahweh reigns forever; he has established his throne for judgment. He will judge the world in righteousness; he will govern the peoples with justice. Do not forget that Creator Yahweh is a refuge for the oppressed, a stronghold in times of trouble. Find your peace in the shadow of his great wings.

Trust in Creator Yahweh, for he has never forsaken those who seek his face.

Eagle People...Today's reading is Psalm 9:1-10.
Pleya gi. "Go with Blessings."

January 29

The Way of Darkness

Warriors, this is the message of walking in beauty, of walking the Spirit Way. Creator Yahweh is Light; in him there is no darkness at all. If we claim to have fellowship with him and yet continue to walk in darkness, we lie and do not live by the truth. But if we walk in the Light, as he is in the Light, we can share the pipe and have fellowship with one another, and the blood of Jesus, his Son, purifies us from all wrong doing. If we claim we have never walked the way of darkness and say we have done no wrong, we deceive ourselves, and the truth is not in us. If we confess our weaknesses and wrong doings, then He is faithful and just and will forgive us our way of error and purify us from all unrighteousness.

My dear warriors, this is what the *Sacred Writings* calls sin. We Natives often call it walking in darkness. Do not walk in darkness. But if anybody does walk in darkness, and at times we all will, we have an advocate with the Father—Jesus Christ, the Righteous One. He is the atoning sacrifice for our sins, and not only for ours but also for the sins of all the tribes of the world.

Eagle People...Today's reading is John 1:1-8.
Pleya gi. "Go with Blessings."

January 30

We Can Know Him!

Don't forget warriors, in the beginning was the Word and the Word was with our Great Chief and Captain. And the Word was our Great Chief and Captain. He was with our Great Chief and Captain in the beginning. Through him (Creator Yahweh) all things were made; without him nothing was made that has been made. This Word, this Jesus Yeshua, is the One our people have long known as Creator. But now we can know him, not only as Creator of all things that we see and do not see, but also as the One who creates new life within our own souls. Now we can know him, not only as The Great Spirit, who is out there somewhere, far beyond us, or someone we meet on the Sacred Mountain of vision quests, but also as The Spirit in whom we live and move and have our being.

Now we can know him, not only as The Spirit who indwells all things, but also as The Holy Spirit who dwells right inside of us. He is the great I Am. He rings out through time, through eternity, through past and future, forever. "I Am"—The Great Spirit, Creator, of whom our forefathers caught a glimpse. "I Am" Creator Yahweh. Jesus. Yeshua. Messiah. Redeemer.

Eagle People...Today's reading is John 1:9-14.
Pleya gi. "Go with Blessings."

January 31

Take Heart!

Warriors, the choice is yours—walk in beauty—or walk in darkness. Creator Yahweh, the true Light that gives Light to everyone, has come into our world.

He was in the world, and though the world was made by him and should have recognized him, they did not. He appeared in the flesh to his own people, but even his own people did not receive him. Yet to all who did and do receive him, to those of us who believe in the name of Jesus Christ Yeshua, he gives the right to become children of Our Great Chief and Captain—children born not of flesh and genealogy, nor of a man or woman's decision or will, but children born of God.

I am writing to you, little children, because you know the Father, our Great Chief and Captain. I write to you, fathers, because you know Creator Yahweh who is from the beginning. I write to you, young warriors, because you are strong, and the Word of Creator Yahweh lives in you, and you have overcome the wicked one, that evil trickster.

Take heart! And continue walking in the way of beauty.

Eagle People...Today's reading is 1 John 2:1-6.
Pleya gi. "Go with Blessings.

Richard Twiss

February

February 1

A Soul Set Free!

Do not fear choosing to walk in beauty, warriors, for it means that you can dance, without feathers or music, in a cell with hard stone for a floor, or completely in the recesses of your mind. You can dance your prayers to Creator Yahweh, knowing he accepts them for what they are—a true offering of praise and love for the One who has given you life. Even when your old, weak legs no longer work, you can close your eyes and dance.

Listen to Creator Yahweh's drumbeat as stone walls fall away and you are transported through a vision to open fields where you dance with all your might. Let the smell of ripe grain and sweet tobacco wrap itself around you, replacing despair with hope and strengthening your body with courage.

When at last you close your eyes and rest on your bed, your thoughts will turn to wonder. If you had never tasted such bitterness; if you had never fallen into the deep pit, you may have missed the sweetness of a soul set free.

Now you are ready for whatever battle waits ahead. Ultimately that battle is in Creator Yahweh's hands, and he is forever faithful. Let such knowledge carry your heart into peaceful rest.

Eagle People...Today's reading is Psalm 37:1-4.
Pleya gi. "Go with Blessings."

21

February 2

Stay Strong!

Stay strong warriors! Continue in faith and keep walking in the Spirit Way. I am writing to you, dear children, because your wrongdoing has been forgiven because of Jesus Yeshua's name. I am writing to you, fathers, because you know Creator Yahweh who is from the beginning. I am writing to you, young warriors, because you have overcome the wicked one, that evil trickster.

Stay strong! Creator Yahweh is the One of whom the disciples said in 1 John 1:1-4 (NIV), "That which was from the beginning, which we have heard, which we have seen with our eyes, which we have looked at and our hands have touched—this we proclaim concerning the Word of life. The life appeared! We have seen it and testify to it, and we proclaim to you the eternal Life, which was with the Father and has appeared to us. We proclaim to you what we have seen and heard, so that you also may have fellowship with us. And our fellowship is with the Father and with his Son, Jesus Christ. We write this to make our joy complete." Stay strong, warriors, and continue walking in the Spirit Way.

Eagle People...Today's reading is 1 John 2:7-14.
Pleya gi. "Go with Blessings."

February 3

When Our Hearts Condemn Us

Warriors, this is how we know we are still walking the way of beauty, that we belong to the truth, and how we set our hearts at rest in Creator Yahweh's presence: If our hearts condemn us, we know that Creator Yahweh is greater than our hearts, and he knows everything.

Warriors, if our hearts do not condemn us, we can come freely before Creator Yahweh and receive anything we ask of him, because we please him by obeying his commands to believe in the name of his Son, Jesus Christ, Yeshua, and to love one another. The one who continues on the way of beauty and keeps Creator Yahweh's commands lives in him, and he in them. We know he lives in us by the power of the Holy Spirit he gave us. Yahweh. Yahweh. Yahweh. Holy is his name!

Eagle People...Today's reading is 1 John 2:15-17.
Pleya gi. "Go with Blessings."

February 4

Choices

My heart jumps at the realization that my Great Chief and Captain is my life and light. No darkness can hide his Light; no walls are strong enough to keep him away, even when I hear the echo of the evil one's footsteps through the dark night. The *Sacred Writings* give me strength where once I was weak. Wisdom from my own people weaves itself through the words.

There was a time our people walked in the true way, the way of walking in beauty, the way of Creator, Yahweh. Long before foreign people brought fences and walls to this land. This is the true strength of the warrior, not with shield and sword, but with a heart bursting with strong medicine and filled with the Spirit of Creator Yahweh.

With this assurance you can feel Creator Yahweh's presence in any and all dark places, the places that are able to rob you of your soul if you allow it.

The choice is yours—walk in beauty—or walk in darkness.

Eagle People...Today's reading is 1 John 2:18-25.
Pleya gi. "Go with Blessings."

February 5

Time is Short

What pain are you in warrior? Death and illness and the loss of dreams have a way of halting a human's purpose. It's easy to wonder for what purpose have we been set here in this time and place. Is there a reason beyond our own understanding?

Suffering reminds us that time is short, that what we hold dear will soon be gone. Yet, even when our hearts fail us we can still soar on eagle wings, for few can walk with a haughty step when sorrow bends the shoulders. Creator Yahweh has a reason beyond our own understanding, and He promises peace beyond as well. Take it to prayer.

Take it to Creator Yahweh. He knows. He understands...even when we do not.

Eagle People...Today's reading is Colossians 1:15-20.
Pleya gi. "Go with Blessings."

February 6

Get Through This

In 2009 the VA called and just so matter of fact over a phone simply said, "You have Hodgkin's." I can't explain the shock. But after a million things ran through my head, I began to tell my wife that we can get through this. We have our Lord and He's a healing Father.

So what do we do? We take it to prayer. If Creator Yahweh heals me on this side, then we accept that. If he takes me home, then I will be healed completely! What loss have you experienced? Take it to Creator Yahweh. He cares. You can get through this. Creator Yahweh is bigger! Creator Yahweh is beyond!

Eagle People...Today's reading is 1 Peter 4:12-16.
Pleya gi. "Go with Blessings."

February 7

Unexpected Places

Warriors, do you find yourself in a world of gray asphalt and concrete, where people come and go without notice of the scent of green on the wind? Neither do they take heed of the gift of warmth from the sun that pierces through the clouded sky?

Stop! Take a moment to see Creator Yahweh in the unexpected places. Take time to remember the One who shut up the sea behind doors. When it burst forth from the womb. Creator Yahweh said, "This far you may come and no farther; here is where your proud waves halt." Job 38:11 (NIV) Take heart, warriors, the One who commands the waves is able to keep you in his mighty hand. When you focus on him, the world of gray disappears.

Eagle People...Today's reading is is Colossians 2:6-10.
Pleya gi. "Go with Blessings."

February 8

Beyond Our Understanding

Warriors, have you considered how great is Creator Yahweh? He is beyond our understanding, yet closer than a blood brother. He calls us by our secret name that only He knows. Creator Yahweh has journeyed to the springs of the sea and walked in the recesses of the deep. He is the One who bound the beautiful Pleiades and loosed the cords of Orion. He brought forth the constellations in their seasons and led out the Bear with its cubs.

When you gaze into the stars, warriors, think about this amazing love, this amazing Creator. Who am I, oh my Great Chief and Captain, that you would pay mind of me? Yahweh. Yahweh. Yahweh.

Eagle People...Today's reading is Colossians 2:20-23.
Pleya gi. "Go with Blessings."

February 9

Life-Giving Breath

Warrior, do you know how important it is to take time each day to be still before Creator Yahweh? Pray. Read the *Sacred Writings,* and then close your eyes and let him work the healing process. Offer every part of your body to the One who breathed life into your lungs.

There is a place for man's medicine, but the soul of you needs much more. Feel Creator Yahweh's life-giving breath trickling into your fingers and toes, then back out again, running up your arms and legs, crossing through your loins and chest and coming to rest in your bruised and battered heart. No drug can match the wonder of this healing caress. No heat can match its soothing breath. He is your Creator and Father, and he loves you more than any human ever can.

Eagle People...Today's reading is Psalm 139:1-6.
Pleya gi. "Go with Blessings."

February 10

Rebirthing Hope

There is a time, warriors, when we must confess our betrayal—telling the truth to the One who already knows it all. This is the act of our betrayal—the thoughts that are less than pleasing to Creator Yahweh; the actions that speak of an attachment to evil; the unlove that invades our souls; the lack of faith with which we betray ourselves.

Though Creator Yahweh knows our every thought before we think it, there is a healing that happens through our confession. And though we may expect rightfully earned condemnation, Creator Yahweh gives us love instead.

Get close to the earth, sit still, and wait, until you are aware of the washing of the Holy Spirit spreading throughout your body, quickening the deadest members and rebirthing hope. Let this awareness swell up inside of you until it bubbles over in waves of joy.

Eagle People...Today's reading is Psalm 139:7-10.
Pleya gi. "Go with Blessings."

February 11

Spiritual Energy

Be alert warriors! We have a very real enemy who prowls around seeking every opportunity to devour us. He comes to rob, steal, kill and destroy. Sometimes he's after our dreams. Sometimes it's our faith. Sometimes it's our very lives. Always it begins in the heart.

This is a time to exercise true spiritual energy. First we choose to believe that Creator Yahweh is in control and that his ways are always good. This is what we call faith. Next we abide in his love through the power of his Holy Spirit and remember that he is greater than our hearts whenever our hearts deceive us. These actions will help us remain steadfast and courageous in our walk with him when the ravenous wolves of worry and doubt threaten to undo us.

Eagle People...Today's reading is 1 Peter 5-6-11.
Pleya gi. "Go with Blessings."

February 12

Shifting Shadows

If one lives long enough they will see the shifting shadows that darken Creator Yahweh's smile. Often we put those shadows there by not taking our Great Chief and Captain at his Word. We keep asking for life's difficulties to be taken away when he has promised us enough grace to keep moving forward. Like the Israelites of ancient days, we get distracted and run in circles waiting for the barriers to be removed.

It is in these times that we must keep moving forward as if there are no obstacles at all. For it is when we step into the rushing waters that he cuts off the flow and makes a way for us to cross on dry ground. Yes. If one lives long enough they will see the shifting shadows that darken Creator Yahweh's smile, but they will also see the light of life that sprouts out of those dark places.

Eagle People...Today's reading is 1 Peter 4:1-11.
Pleya gi. "Go with Blessings."

February 13

The Joy of Your Heart

Be careful warriors that no one entices you with the object of your dreams, for the promise of power may turn you aside from walking in beauty. Seek Creator Yahweh before all else. Let him be the object of your dreams. His word is eternal; it stands firm in the heavens. His faithfulness continues through all generations; he established the earth, and it endures.

Are you afflicted? Let Creator Yahweh's law be your delight and you will not perish in your affliction. Never forget his precepts, for by them our lives are renewed. His *Sacred Writings* show us the path where our moccasins should tread. They warn us when we go astray and call us back into walking the way of Beauty. Let his Word be a lamp to your feet and a light for your path. This will be the joy of your heart.

Eagle People...Today's reading is
1 John 5:21 & Psalm 119:89-112.
Pleya gi. "Go with Blessings."

February 14

Wonder & Delight

Warriors, sometimes the path seems long, too long, as we make our way toward the Sacred Mountain, and we may grow weary and give up if it weren't for the fact that Creator Yahweh is the One who leads us, and Creator Yahweh is our Father who loves us more than anyone else ever can. That is an eternal truth that the oldest and youngest believer, alike, may grasp, and once we do, even while crossing through the churning waters, we can rest in the faith that He will lead us safely to the goal.

Arthur Christopher Bacon says it well, "I still believe that a day of understanding will come for each of us, however far away it may be. We will understand as we see the tragedies that today darken and dampen the presence of heaven for us take their proper place in God's great plan—a plan so overwhelming, magnificent, and joyful, we will laugh with wonder and delight." Let us purpose to find wonder and delight in the unexpected moments of each day.

Eagle People...Today's reading is Matthew 6:25-34.
Pleya gi. "Go with Blessings."

February 15

Beyond The Stars

Warriors, do not forget that Creator Yahweh's love endures forever, and he does not abandon the works of his hands. He knows our frame that we are but dust; he knows what thoughts dwell inside each of us; he knows how far short our thoughts fall of his holiness.

Creator Yahweh is exalted far beyond the stars, beyond the Bear and the Cub, yet he looks kindly on the lowly. He knows your frame is but dust, yet even in your weakness his strength is made perfect. Let us dance and sing of the ways of our Great Chief and Captain for his glory is very great. His faithfulness never ceases. Yahweh. Yahweh. Yahweh.

Eagle People...Today's reading is Psalm 138.
Pleya gi. "Go with Blessings."

February 16

Wallowing with The Pigs

In today's Eagle People reading, Creator Yahweh tells us about a man who had two sons. One stayed home and was obedient and faithful to his father while the youngest took his share of his father's estate and went off and squandered it. But, one day, he came to his senses. Have you experienced a day like that in your life? Where you came to your senses? Where you realized that you were wallowing with the pigs?

I know this life. I once walked the way of deep sorrow. Then I came to my senses and began calling out to Creator Yahweh. Day after day, I called out to Creator Yahweh and never gave up. I walked the land and holy ground below the Sacred Mountain and called his name. I cried. I pleaded. And finally, he heard the cry of this broken, battered Vietnam vet, and I began to crawl down the way of faithfulness, moving forward in the love of my Great Chief and Captain.

Walk on, warriors. Crawl on! Slowly though it may be. Creator Yahweh does not stay up on the Sacred Mountain. He is very near. He hears your cry for mercy.

Eagle People...Today's reading is Luke 15:11-32.
Pleya gi. "Go with Blessings."

February 17

Pride in The Way

Creator Yahweh tells another story of a young man who is broken and paralyzed and how four of his friends decided they would take him to Jesus Yeshua. But the crowd was so great and dense that the friends couldn't even get through the door to the place where Jesus was talking.

That's how I felt when I walked day after day below the Sacred Mountain. It seemed the crowd of liars in my mind was too great and I could not break through.

In Creator Yahweh's story, these four brave men lifted their paralyzed brother up, stretcher and all, and broke through the thatched roof. Then they lowered him down to Jesus Yeshua. That's what happened to me. Creator Yahweh sent a brave sister and her friend who carried me to Jesus. Through their help, I was able to stand and walk slowly into the way of faithfulness.

You may be a brave warrior or highly respected council member, but don't let pride get in the way. There is a time to admit your brokenness and accept help, but take caution, warriors, accept only the help that comes through Creator Yahweh. Sometimes it comes in the strangest forms.

Eagle People...Today's reading is Mark 2:1-12.
Pleya gi. "Go with Blessings."

February 18

A Broken Man

Yesterday, I mentioned that sometimes Creator Yahweh's help comes in the strangest forms. My first help came in a way I least expected. Creator Yahweh tells a story of this kind of help where a man was robbed and left to die along the side of the road. All the people you would expect to help passed him by, but the last person in the world you would have thought would help, not only stopped, but lifted the broken man to his own donkey and walked him to a safe place. There he paid for his lodging and meals until the broken man was able to get on his feet again.

My first help came when I was ready to end it all, through a stepfather I had hated with everything in me. He not only got in his truck and drove many long miles to get me, but he did so with one leg, since he had been very recently released from the hospital following amputation.

Don't be surprised, warriors, if your help comes from such an unexpected place. Do not despise the day of small things. Bask in the peace that only Creator Yahweh can give. Receive the healing that reaches past skin and bones!

Eagle People...Today's reading is Luke 10:25-35.
Pleya gi. "Go with Blessings."

February 19

Falling Like Rain

We are tribal people are we not? Yes. There is a time for solitude, a time for vision quest, a time for healing. But there is also a time to join with our people to encourage and strengthen. We are to encourage with the encouragement that we have been given; to comfort with the comfort we've been given. We do not need to wait until we are elders to share this blessing. Creator Yahweh's blessings come from the first moment that our hearts sing out to him.

Do you know someone who has just come to their senses as we talked about on February 16 in the story of the two sons? We once came to our senses, now it is time to help someone else as Holy Spirit brings them to their senses, but be careful warrior, do not return to the way of temptation. Stay away from whatever road will take you there.

Perhaps a fishing trip, a horse ride, or a walk up the Sacred Mountain. Perhaps beading regalia, painting a drum, or singing over a drum. Take the *Sacred Writings* with you. Hide its words in your heart. Let them fall like rain from the heavens. You will discover that you are blessed and comforted and encouraged as much and more as the one you are lifting up to Creator Yahweh.

Eagle People...Today's reading is 2 Corinthians 1:3-7.
Pleya gi. "Go with Blessings."

February 20

Prisoners of Darkness

Warriors, sometimes the way before us grows so dark that sorrow falls like fog. Darkness slips over our path and evil slinks through the forest. We can smell its foul odor and hear padding feet. Then doubt fills the hollow places in our souls. In these times, Creator Yahweh seems far away, but he is not.

In these times it is important to cry out to him, even if all you can muster is a sigh. Direct your sigh at him, he will hear. For he is the One the *Sacred Writings* speak of when they say, "The Spirit of the Sovereign LORD is upon me, because the LORD has anointed me to proclaim good news to the poor." Isaiah 61:1 (NIV)

Many of us who continue to walk the Sorrow Way are poor in spirit and in great need of this good news. The news that Creator Yahweh has come to bind up the brokenhearted, to proclaim freedom for the captives and release from darkness for prisoners. Often we are such prisoners of darkness that we fail to see when the fog begins to lift. But lift it will, warriors, if you wait upon Creator Yahweh. He will bind your broken heart and renew your strength. You need do no more than this, simply wait, simply sigh. Yahweh. Yahweh. Yahweh.

Eagle People…Today's reading is Isaiah 61:1-3.
Pleya gi. "Go with Blessings."

February 21

No Deep Shadow

Does the way still seem dark, warriors? Perhaps it is even more frightening than before. It is hard to see now, but there is still a future and a hope. It will come to you in good time, though it does not seem like it now. Creator Yahweh will anoint you with the oil of joy instead of mourning. He will save you from the fowler's snare

I know the beast of sorrow seems enormous and overpowering, but the beast has already been defeated. Already your Redeemer is on his way. Still it is okay to weep, to mourn for your loss. Jesus Yeshua, too, wept and he still grieves over the loss of his children.

You are his beloved child. He will not let you go. There is no dark place, no deep shadow that is so dark that Creator Yahweh's light cannot fill it.

Eagle People...Today's reading is Isaiah 61:4-7.
Pleya gi. "Go with Blessings."

February 22

A Hope & A Future

Warriors, a day will come when we will look back and see that during those times when we were weak and our hearts were full of sorrow, that Creator Yahweh carried us on eagle's wings. If we would but rest in him we might know the supreme joy of such flight even in the midst of great trial. This is not the joy that bubbles up in laughter, but the joy that wells deep in our souls and brings a glimmer of hope. Hope is like faith, based on real evidence and sure as if the thing sought has already been realized.

This joy we can hang onto, this hope, this faith, because the One who gives it is our Savior, Jesus, Yeshua. He is the Creator who has given us all good things as well as a hope and a future, an eternity free of sorrow and pain. In this world we will have trouble, but take heart, Creator Yahweh has overcome the world.

Eagle People...Today's reading is John 14:1-14.
Pleya gi. "Go with Blessings."

February 23

Beneath His Wings

Yes, warriors, in this world you will have trouble, but in the spiritual realm, the place where eternal battles are won, Creator Yahweh covers you with his feathers. Spend time there, as you take refuge beneath his wings. Let his faithfulness, which remains even when we are faithless, be your shield and rampart.

If you do this in the spiritual realm, then his peace will follow you back to this world, and you will not fear the terror of padding feet at night, nor the arrow that flies by day, nor the pestilence that stalks in the darkness, nor the plague that destroys at noon. These things may strike down this body but they cannot touch the soul, that part of us that flies on eagle's wings. Let your soul find rest in Creator Yahweh alone. He alone is your rock and your salvation. Trust in him at all times. Pour out your heart to him.

Eagle People...Today's reading is Psalm 91:1-8.
Pleya gi. "Go with Blessings."

February 24

Battlefield of the Mind

In this world, warriors, the enemy may press you hard and fast against a stone mountain, but Creator Yahweh will not allow the evil trickster to crush your spirit beyond repair. The enemy may confuse and bewilder you, but Creator Yahweh will not allow him to drop your soul into a place of complete hopelessness.

Our Great Chief and Captain will give you hope in the darkest of dark places, in the battlefield of the mind, where the enemy speaks lies that we believe. Listen for his voice there, in that dark place, as he gives instruction. Fill your mind with the *Sacred Writings.*

Yes. Creator Yahweh may allow us to undergo much persecution, but he will never abandon us. He will be with us in the secret place where no one can touch our souls. Yes, some of us will be struck down, but Creator Yahweh will never allow us to be destroyed. He stands with open arms to receive us. Precious in his sight is the death of one of his servants. Yahweh. Yahweh. Yahweh. He is the lover of our souls.

Eagle People...Today's reading is 2 Corinthians 4:1-6.
Pleya gi. "Go with Blessings."

February 25

Jars of Clay

Do not lose heart, warriors. We hold this great treasure of Creator Yahweh in jars of clay. That is what we are, jars of clay, broken and holding nothing but darkness. But Creator Yahweh said, "Let light shine out of darkness!" And he made his light shine in our hearts. In doing so he gave us the light of the knowledge of his glory in the face of Christ. We find this knowledge of Light in the *Sacred Writings*. This Light is the One we knew all along as Creator. Now this Light fills all our dark places. That's why we hold this treasure in jars of clay, to show that this all-surpassing power is from Creator Yahweh and not from us. We always carry around in our body the death of Jesus Yeshua, so that the life of Jesus Yeshua may also be revealed in our body.

Eagle People...Today's reading is 2 Corinthians 4:7-12.
Pleya gi. "Go with Blessings."

February 26

Enemy of Our Souls

Make the Most High your dwelling. Let Creator Yahweh be your refuge. Because you love Creator Yahweh, he will rescue you. Because you acknowledge his name, he will protect you from the second death, the true enemy of our souls. Call upon him and he will answer. He will be with you in trouble.

In the spiritual realm, that place where warriors fight great battles, you will tread upon the lion and the cobra; you will trample the great lion and the serpent. Because you love Creator Yahweh and make him your dwelling place, no disaster will come near your tent. For he will command his angels concerning you to guard you in all your ways. They will lift you up in their hands, so that you will not strike your foot against a stone. Your body and emotions may take a hit, but your soul will be safe if you make Creator Yahweh your dwelling place.

Eagle People...Today's reading is Psalm 91:9-16.
Pleya gi. "Go with Blessings."

February 27

Stand Back!

Have you lost sight of the goal, warriors? Has the enemy of our souls convinced you that such a prize is unreachable? Cha-aat! Tell him to stand back! All you need is one glimpse of

Creator Yahweh's face. He rides on the wings of the wind, coming from that far off place to meet with you.

Listen! The thunder of Creator Yahweh's voice rings through the heavens! He will draw you out of the water. He will deliver you from certain death and set you on your feet. Earth will become solid and strong beneath your feet until you borrow its strength and it becomes your own.

Wait for Creator Yahweh. He will come. Indeed, he is already here, right in the depths of your heart. Let his deep, unquenchable love fill every part of you, restoring your soul and replacing despair with hope. Yahweh. Yahweh. Yahweh. Let his whispered command fill your ears, "Stand firm I AM with you."

Eagle People...Today's reading is Psalm 18:1-19.
Pleya gi. "Go with Blessings."

February 28

Fully Native, Fully Christian

There are many voices, warriors. Be careful which ones your ears take in. I've heard it said that we Natives should not believe in Jesus Yeshua, because in so doing we will give the white man the satisfaction of thinking he has won. This same voice cautions to not allow our children to be absorbed in religions.

I have much to say about this, but I will keep my words few. First of all, to think that Jesus Yeshua belongs to the white man is in error. Read the *Sacred Writings.* You will see this is no white man's God. This is Yahweh, Creator, the One we have been worshipping all along. Don't allow the wrong doing of any man or woman keep you from the truth. Creator Yahweh has given us his words, which are rich to live by and good for correction. Sit close to the earth and absorb his words into your soul.

My people are fully Native and fully Christian, but do not confuse that with white traditions. We use our regalia, language, dancing, and customs in our worship of Creator, and in doing so, we have felt Creator Yahweh's pleasure and delight. These practices are bringing much honor to our people and restoring our dignity.

We welcome our white friends to worship with us, not in a contest of who will win or lose, but as members of one Tribe, many nations coming together under Creator Yahweh.

Eagle People...Today's reading is Galatians 3:23-29. *Pleya gi.* "Go with Blessings."

Laura Grabner
(Ghostdancer's mother)

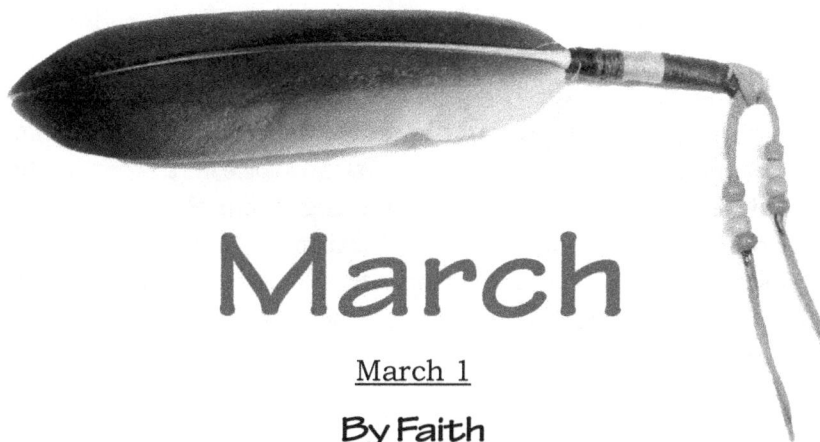

March

By Faith

Warriors, have you considered what it means to have faith? Now faith is being sure of what we hope for and certain of what we do not see. It has long been easy for us to believe by faith that everything we see and don't see was formed at Creator Yahweh's command, so that what is seen was not made out of what is visible.

This is the same, Creator Yahweh, who loads the clouds with water and weeps upon the earth. At his direction they swirl and do whatever he commands, sometimes bringing justice; other times showing his great love as he waters the face of the earth. By faith we learn to trust him, so that when he answers our prayers differently than what we hoped, we understand by faith that what we receive is what we would have asked for if we knew as much as he does about the situation. This is the kind of faith that will carry us through the path of sorrow and onto the Beauty Way.

Eagle People...Today's reading is Hebrews 11:1-16.

Pleya gi. "Go with Blessings."

March 2

Dance Your Prayers!

Praise Creator Yahweh with all of your heart! Stand beneath the night sky with your arms lifted to heaven and sing his praise. Bow down to the earth and savor his sweetness. Dance your prayers before him. For his love and his faithfulness are unfailing. His glory beyond understanding.

Our people should have been the first to recognize Yahweh as Creator, this Jesus Yeshua who laid down his life for us. We saw him in the sunrise over the Sacred Mountain. We heard him in the wapiti's bugle, and we watched him dance in the flight of nighthawks.

Stand still and listen. Creator Yahweh's voice is heard in all the earth! We live and move and have our being in him. Such knowledge is enough to make your feet move to the drum of his heartbeat. What problems do we have that he cannot fix? What enemies can he not defeat? Praise Creator Yahweh for he will not abandon the works of his hands.

Eagle People...Today's reading is Psalm 139:11-12.
Pleya gi. "Go with Blessings."

March 3

A Place for You!

Warriors, who let the wild donkey go free? Who untied his ropes? Creator Yahweh gave him the vast wilderness as his home. He roams the earth free from restraint or a driver's shout. He laughs at the commotion in cities and towns. Distant hills are his pasture with not one fence to hold him in. He searches for any green thing and finds it, because Creator Yahweh provides for all his needs.

Warrior, do you think you are of any less value than the wild donkey? Our Great Chief and Captain is preparing a place for you! And even now, he provides for all your soul's needs.

Be content in whatever circumstances you find yourself in. Thank him for the gift of breath. Focus on all good things he has blessed you with and let your heart delight in his unfailing love. Then let this love flow through you to everyone you meet and never give up asking the question, "How can love reign in this place?"

Eagle People...Today's reading is Psalm 13:8-10.
Pleya gi. "Go with Blessings."

March 4

Forget The Former Things!

L et us straighten up, warriors, and set ourselves back on the beautiful way. If we repent, Creator Yahweh will restore us so that we may serve him. Forget the former things! Do not dwell on the past. Our Great Chief and Captain is doing a new thing! Now it springs up; do you not see and understand? He is making a way in the desert and streams in the wilderness to give refreshment to his people, the people he created for himself. He does this so that we may proclaim his praise.

Do not be afraid; you have been chosen. Creator Yahweh will pour water on the thirsty land, and streams on the dry ground. He will pour out his Spirit on our offspring and his blessing on our descendants. They will spring up like grass in a meadow, like poplar trees by flowing streams. Let us repent and follow the way of beauty.

Eagle People...Today's reading is Romans 13:11-14.
Pleya gi. "Go with Blessings."

March 5

He Made The Stars!

A re you confident in what you hope for, warriors? If not, perhaps you are hoping for the wrong thing. Or perhaps your confidence is in the wrong thing. Our confidence is best found in Creator Yahweh, believing that if we had all the facts he has we would be asking for what he has given us.

Creator Yahweh knows the future. He knows what lives inside of us. Faith is confidence in what we hope for and assurance of what our eyes do not see. Our people have long used faith to believe that the universe was formed at Creator Yahweh's command, believing that what we see was not made out of what was visible.

By faith Abraham, when called to leave his family land and travel to a place he knew nothing about, a place that he would later receive as his inheritance, obeyed and went, even though he did not know where he was going. We know we are traveling, like Abraham, toward our inheritance, but we do not know the steps that will lead us there. Remain in faith, dear warrior. Remain in love. It is not your hard work that will get you to that land. It is Creator Yahweh's work in you. Rest in him. Move only when he commands. Trust Him. He has earned your trust. He made the stars!

Eagle People...Today's reading is Hebrews 11:17-40.
Pleya gi. "Go with Blessings."

March 6

Silence The Liars!

Warriors do you need to silence the mouths of liars? Then, earnestly seek Creator Yahweh. Long for him as one who is crossing a hot desert where there is no water. Let your soul thirst for him. Get close to the earth and read the *Sacred Writings.* Eat his words. They will be like honey for your soul.

Let your soul be satisfied with Creator Yahweh as with the richest of foods. Look up to the heavens and see. Behold his power and his great glory! Lift up your hands and your heart to him. His love is better than life; let it wash over you in cleansing waves. Command your soul to cling to him. Rest in the assurance that his right hand upholds you above your earthly circumstances. Remember him throughout the long watches of the night.

Creator Yahweh is your help! Sing in the shadow of his wings. Dance your prayers before him. Rejoice in your Creator! Your rejoicing will silence the mouths of liars. Yahweh. Yahweh. Yahweh.

Eagle People...Today's reading is Psalm 63.
Pleya gi. "Go with Blessings."

March 7

The Power of Brokeness

Even warriors shed tears. And when we do, we often feel as helpless as a deer caught in the headlamps of a vehicle. Tears are a foreign thing to us. When you shed tears, let yourself go. Place your life completely in Creator Yahweh's mercy. Let him do with you what he wants. This is better than complaining about our circumstances or demanding an audience to state our case.

The strength of which we were once so proud will seem but a small thing when we have experienced the power of brokenness at Creator Yahweh's feet. We may think it great that we call ourselves horse whisperers, but Creator Yahweh knows the language of trees. we may be proud to ride bareback across open fields, but He rides the wings of wind. Can you tame wild horses? He commands the wind and storm.

Surely we thought and spoke of things we did not understand, things too wonderful for us to know. Creator Yahweh is above and beyond and exalted in power. In His justice and great righteousness, He does not oppress. We are in the presence of The Almighty. How dare we stand on our feet?

Eagle People...Today's reading is Job 42:1-6.
Pleya gi. "Go with Blessings."

March 8

Warriors of Old

A wise man, John Henry Jowett, once wrote, "Evil never surrenders its grasp without a tremendous fight." This is something we spiritual warriors should never forget. The warriors of old knew this. They were not arrogant in their interpretation of the *Sacred Writings.* They knew blood would be shed, dreams forsaken, and heights left unclaimed. Jowett went on to write, "Satan is not put to flight by our courteous request. He completely blocks our way, and our progress must be recorded in blood and tears."

Our people know much about blood and tears, as every true believer in Creator Yahweh must know. Most of us took our first breaths in this world under the protection of clean and protected surroundings. Not so when we are born of Spirit. Spirit knows no walls. Being born of Spirit means open skies where we "draw our strength from the distress of the storm." Buffeting winds and howling wolves welcome us to a dangerous world.

"We must go through many hardships to enter the kingdom of God."

Eagle People...Today's reading is Job 34:10-15.
Pleya gi. "Go with Blessings."

March 9

What is in Your Hand?

Warrior, what is in your hand? Do you hold a spear? Then fight bravely! But remember that the battle is not of flesh and blood. The battle is fought in the Spirit where the Word of Creator Yahweh is the most powerful weapon.

Do you hold an instrument? Then play joyfully with all your heart! Sing songs that help bring others to restoration. Do you hold a tool? Then work with all your might and skill, making the way better for others. Do you hold words? Then write words of encouragement and truth that will bring life and not death to your readers. Do you hold a paintbrush? Then let your paint spill into glorious creations that speak of Creator Yahweh's wonder.

Do you hold nothing? Then open your hands to your Great Chief and Captain and let him fill them with his great, unfailing love. Keep them open and raise them up so that his love flows over you and everyone you meet. Whatever may be in your hand, work at it with all your soul to the glory of Creator Yahweh and not for men.

Eagle People...Today's reading is Colossians 3:1-4.
Pleya gi. "Go with Blessings."

March 10

Confess The Darkness

Dear warrior, if Creator Yahweh stood before you right now, would you tremble? Or would you celebrate? If you would celebrate, then celebrate now! Dance your prayers before him. Lift up your voice in praise! Honor him with your song.

But if you would tremble, then tremble now. Confess the darkness of the recesses of your heart. Put to death, whatever belongs to the old nature...any of those practices that Creator Yahweh would not choose to bless. Kill the evil desires lurking in your members... those animal impulses and appetites. Don't allow any lustful thing to stay long in front of your eyes.

Get rid of anger, rage, and bad feelings toward others. Put away and rid yourself of foulmouthed abuse, filthy language and shameful communication such as cursing and slandering others from your lips. Get rid of greed and evil desires, which lead you into idolatry. Do not lie to anyone. You used to walk in these ways, when you were living in darkness and were addicted to such practices, but do so no longer. Walk the Beauty Way and you will find rest for your soul.

Eagle People...Today's reading is Colossians 3:5-11.
Pleya gi. "Go with Blessings."

March 11

People of Joy!

Creator Yahweh does speak—now one way, now another—though we may not perceive it. In a dream, in a vision of the night, when deep sleep overtakes us, Creator Yahweh may whisper in our ears. Let us listen for his voice and let ourselves be known for speaking truth and encouragement. Let us be people of joy! Let us practice kindness. We have taken off the old self and started walking the Spirit Way.

Through the power of Holy Spirit, let us leave behind those old practices that once held us in chains. Let us not run in circles but let us walk steadily forward, one step at a time, following Creator Yahweh who has gone before. Then, when we see him we will no longer tremble in fear. Our souls will soar like an eagle in celebration of the great love of our Great Chief and Captain!

Eagle People...Today's reading is
Job 33:1-33 and 34:1-4.
Pleya gi. "Go with Blessings."

March 12

You Were in His Mind

Look at the heavens and see. Do they not declare the glory of Creator Yahweh! Stare intently from east to west, from north to south. Examine all between. Memorize every detail. No matter how hard you stare or intently you study you will never hold the whole picture in your mind. Yet Creator Yahweh held all this and more in his mind before he spoke the Word to make it become.

He also held YOU in his mind. He knew you BEFORE the foundation of the world. Before time. Before he spoke the universe into existence. Before the heavens! He saw YOU. Every part of you. The good, the bad, and the ugly. He knew your name, and he called. YOU.

From earth our bodies came, and to earth we will return, but our souls were breathed by HIM! And He calls us to return. Listen! The sound of his voice thunders! Answer the call of our Great Chief and Captain and walk the Spirit Way.

Eagle People...Today's reading is Ephesians 1:3-14
Pleya gi. "Go with Blessings."

March 13

Chosen People

Have you answered the call of Creator Yahweh? Then you are one of his chosen people, holy and dearly loved. Let his regalia of compassion fall over you and hide your nakedness. Let humility be your headdress, and gentleness the fan that waves sweet peace over all who are near.

Shod your feet with the moccasins of patience that you may bear whatever grievances you have with your brothers and sisters. Forgive as Creator Yahweh has forgiven you, without asking for anything in return. And over all of this, pull on a blanket of love that will bind you together as one tribe in perfect unity. Our Great Chief and Captain has given us but two commands: To love him and to love others. Let us walk in the way of love.

Eagle People...Today's reading is Colossians 3:12-14.
Pleya gi. "Go with Blessings."

March 14

Rhythm of Gratitude

Warriors, let the peace and soul harmony of Creator Yahweh rule in your hearts. As chosen ones, we have all been called to walk in the way of peace, not in sadness with our heads down but with thankful hearts and singing lips, dancing and singing the words of our Great Chief and Captain.

Allow gratitude to ring in every drumbeat as you match it to Creator Yahweh's heart. Beat out the rhythm of gratitude. Let the melody of grace take root in your soul. Let the word spoken by Christ, the Messiah, Creator Yahweh, those words we call the *Sacred Writings,* have its home in your hearts and minds and make its dwelling place in you.

Speak the Word. Dance the Word. Love the Word. Walk the Word. Bathe in the Word. Let it cleanse you and make you whole and restore you. Make melody to Jesus Yeshua with grace in your hearts.

Eagle People...Today's reading is Colossians 3:15-17.
Pleya gi. "Go with Blessings."

March 15

How Deep is His Love!

Healing is found in Creator Yahweh's love. Restoration is in his love. Life eternal. How deep is his love! How wide. If you have reached out your hands to the heavens and accepted his love, then there is no place your feet trod that you will not step in his love. He keeps you, he restores you by his love.

Nothing comes between you and Creator Yahweh's love. What troubles do you have? What hardship? What persecution? His love still flows over you. If you are hungry or naked, his love is still there.

Arrows fly! Danger threatens! Yet his blanket of love still covers you. Death and life do not change his love. Heavenly messengers may tempt you, dark spirits may threaten, but they do not change his love. His love remains in the present, in the future. It stands against spiritual power. There is nothing so high that his love cannot reach, no pit so low that his love does not fill. Nothing in the present, in the future, in all creation can come between Creator Yahweh's anointed and his love.

Let the healing begin. Light and dark meet in Creator Yahweh's love. His eternal love reached into the future and saw you! He chose you! He called you by name.

Eagle People...Today's reading is Romans 8:1-17.
Pleya gi. "Go with Blessings."

March 16

In The Midst of Trouble

L et the shout of victory reign! Let the walls fall. Trust Creator Yahweh's love. He will carry us through the storm. Yes, the storm is dangerous. Yes, it is exhausting. But he who shut up the sea behind doors when it burst forth from the womb is with us. He will preserve our lives even when we walk in the midst of trouble.

Our present troubles, though they cause us much suffering, are not worth comparing with the glory that Creator Yahweh will one day reveal in us. All of creation waits in eager expectation for the sons and daughters of God to be revealed! Listen carefully, you will hear the groaning of a vast creation waiting to be liberated. Our hearts groan, as well, longing for the day of perfect freedom.

Take heart warrior. Do you have no words to pray? Even a sigh directed at Creator Yahweh is a prayer. Holy Spirit helps us in our weakness, interceding for us with groans that mere words cannot express. Let Creator Yahweh's love restore you. Shout for joy while hope is still an expectation. Let the shout of victory confuse the enemy's camp. Trust our Great Chief and Captain's love. He will carry us through.

Eagle People...Today's reading is Romans 8:18-27.
Pleya gi. "Go with Blessings."

March 17

Embrace of Heaven

W arrior, when is the last time you felt the embrace of Creator Yahweh? Have you wept for joy in his presence? It is a good thing to take time to be still, get close to the earth and let the embrace of heaven wash over you. Let his sweet caress soothe away every vestige of pain and crushing memories. Know the truth, as Creator Yahweh knows the truth. See deeper than the surface. Allow him to open your eyes to the hearts of others. Let understanding become as common as your breath.

Taking the time to be still before your Great Chief and Captain will help you to stand firm and know that he is with you in the common places of life, the times when you would otherwise feel forsaken of all that is sacred. It is good to stay in touch with the embrace of heaven.

Eagle People...Today's reading is Romans 8:28-39.
Pleya gi. "Go with Blessings."

<u>March 18</u>

Return to Freedom!

Warriors, you were running a good race. Who cut in on you and kept you from obeying the truth? Do not listen to the evil trickster who is throwing you into confusion. You were called to be free. So live in freedom! But not in such a way as to do evil but in such a way that allows you to love others.

Loving Creator Yahweh. Loving others. This is the Spirit Way.

And let us watch our words, they hold the power of life and death. Let us not speak death to one another. Let us not bite and devour one another. Instead, let us walk the Spirit Way and we will not gratify the desires of the old nature. Let us return to freedom. Let us return to the Spirit Way.

Eagle People...Today's reading is Galatians 5:1-26.
Pleya gi. "Go with Blessings."

<u>March 19</u>

The Way of Love

Warriors, remember to walk in the way of love. Love is patient. Love is kind. It always forgives one another. It goes that extra mile. It never fails. It always keeps going and going. This is the love that Creator Yahweh loves us with and it is the love that should spill over our lives as we love one another.

Creator Yahweh's love will never fail. Never! If we think it has failed it is because we have stopped trusting. Stopped believing. Stopped loving. His love NEVER fails. His love always protects. Through His love, we love one another.

His love does not envy. It does not boast. His love is not easily angered. His love reaches out to thousands upon thousands. This love always gives hope. Creator Yahweh's love binds our hearts together. This is the love with which we love each other.

Eagle People...Today's reading is 1 Corinthians 13.
Pleya gi. "Go with Blessings."

March 20

The Grass Dancer Above All!

Warriors, be sure to spend much time in the *Sacred Writings* found in the *Bible*. This is no white man's book as some of our people call it. It is a book of life-giving words given by Creator and passed down from one generation to another, kept alive by prophesies fulfilled hundreds of years after they were first given and fueled by the hope of a Messiah to come. A Messiah, a Great Chief, the Grass Dancer above all grass dancers, who made a Way for His People, the Way of Beauty, the Blessing Way.

Now, we are one great new tribe made up of all who put their trust in Jesus Yeshua, Creator Yahweh.

Read the sacred words of beauty and raise your hands to the sky, calling upon Creator Yahweh, the one who sees, the great counselor, the faithful great "Blaydal'knii" (God above all). Ask him to restore you, for he alone knows your true needs. Dance your prayers to him as you step out each heartbeat of the drum.

Eagle People...Today's reading is John 3:16-21.
Pleya gi. "Go with Blessings."

March 21

Honor One Another

Sisters and brothers do you know that we are joint heirs of Creator Yahweh? That means we are equal heirs. Men be careful in thinking that you should instruct your wife with the *Sacred Writings.* You are joint heirs, you will share the Word together, not instruct one another. Men, don't be a dufus in the Word.

Jesus Yeshua treated women as valuable. Have your hands washed from sin to lift holy hands to Creator Yahweh. These are notes I write to myself. Perhaps they will mean something to you as well. Also, our adornment should be the Word, not fancy threads. Our people have always valued order and respect. As you can see, the *Sacred Writings* are also about order and respect. Our lives are so much richer when we value and honor one another. First of all honor Creator Yahweh, then honor one another. This is the blessing way, the path of Creator Yahweh that leads to a far-seeing place. Here you will find the wellsprings that will quench your thirsty soul.

Eagle People...Today's reading is 1 Timothy 2:1-15.
Pleya gi. "Go with Blessings."

March 22

Like The Stars Forever

Warrior, bring your life to Creator Yahweh. Lean on him, rely on him; place your confidence in him. Sit beside the fire and let him show you his ways. Walk along the path with him, letting him take the lead. Walk in his footsteps while he guides you in truth and faithfulness. He is the God of your salvation.

Do not worry about evil people who seem to prosper in your shame. Their days are but dust; they are here today and gone tomorrow. But you, warrior, will shine like the stars forever, because you have trusted in his great love. Creator Yahweh is good and upright and he will guide you to a spacious place. The way getting there may be dark and lonely, but soon you will dance with all your heart. Never give up trusting in your Great Chief and Captain.

Eagle People...Today's reading is Psalm 25:1-11.
Pleya gi. "Go with Blessings."

March 23

From Days of Old

Evil people will come against you, warriors, but it is not the person who is truly your enemy, it is the evil one, that evil trickster, in the spiritual realm that is out to get you. He has no power over you, except that Creator Yahweh allows. So, lift your petition to your Great Chief and Captain! Call out to him expectantly all the day long. Remember his great mercy and love that never fail. They are from days of old and are everlasting.

He knew you when you walked in rebellious ways, yet he called you to be one of his own. All the ways of Creator Yahweh are loving and faithful toward those who keep his covenant and his testimonies. For his name's sake, he will pardon your iniquity and guilt, even though they are very great. Put your hope in him and he will guard your life and rescue you. All his paths are mercy and unwavering love.

Eagle People...Today's reading is Psalm 25:12-22.
Pleya gi. "Go with Blessings."

March 24

Power of Stillness

Warriors, be careful to not steal tomorrow from the hands of Creator Yahweh. Surely you have learned by now that he is never late. Every great warrior needs time to prepare themselves for battle. Are your hands prepared for war? Is your heart?

Let us prepare our hearts first. It is good to take time for a vision quest, finding a place to be alone with Creator Yahweh, somewhere close to the earth and free of human noise and interference. Perhaps you have a sacred mountain nearby where you can do this, but if it is impossible for you to get to such a place, any place is sacred if Creator Yahweh is invited into it. We live and move and have our being in him. The place we choose is simply for us to become aware of his presence.

For the next few days I will share with you things you can do while upon the mountain (whether that mountain is a quiet place in your home or a lofty peak) to prepare your heart for war. Yes. We are in a war, where the stakes are life and death. Today it is enough for you to think about where your special place will be and to remember that your life is in the hands of our Great Chief and Captain who also holds the future.

Creator Yahweh is not silent as some count as silence. His silence is the power of stillness. Wait for him. His timing is always perfect.

Eagle People...Today's reading is Hebrews 10:1-10.
Pleya gi. "Go with Blessings."

March 25

Your Secret Place

Warriors, there is power in silence. When you are in your secret place (as we talked about yesterday), let silence stretch long until you center and once again regain your foundation. This is the power of rebuilding, with no tool in hand, but with fingers spread and palms open, as the rubble falls away at Creator Yahweh's command. Then you will see a clear foundation on which to build.

This foundation is the heart and center of who you are. This is the foundation that cannot be shaken. This is the foundation built on Creator Yahweh's sacrifice and by which we are being made holy. When all else that can be shaken is shaken, Christ remains.

Think on this when you are in your secret place. Let your heart be encouraged by the work that has already been done for you, spoken when the worlds were set into place by Creator Yahweh's commands. Catch this vision before you catch any other. There is power in silence as you wait for Creator Yahweh. His silence may be long, but it is never late.

Eagle People...Today's reading is Hebrews 10:11-18.
Pleya gi. "Go with Blessings."

March 26

Climb The Sacred Mountain

Remember warrior that faith is the tool that no hand, but Creator Yahweh's, can hold for long. Lay your tiny faith in his mighty hand and watch as he builds something strong, useful and beautiful.

Enter the Most Holy Place by the blood of Jesus Yeshua. Climb the Sacred Mountain, whether in body or in mind. Cleanse yourself with the water of Holy Spirit and with the smoke of sweet burning sage. Draw near to Creator Yahweh with a sincere heart and with full assurance of faith.

He will provide this faith for you, just keep turning to him in each and every moment and circumstance. Let him take your heart and soften it until it can be remolded into a warrior's heart. This is still a time for silence as he remolds you. Wait until you hear his words, "It is finished."

Eagle People...Today's reading is Hebrews 10:19-22.
Pleya gi. "Go with Blessings."

March 27

Creed of The Cross

As spiritual warriors we stand upon the creed of the cross, and we hold unswervingly to the hope we profess. For Creator Yahweh has given us many promises, and he is forever faithful, even when we are faithless. Warriors, in these times, it is easy to see The Day fast approaching, a Day of raging fire that will consume the enemies of our Great Chief and Captain. So now, more than ever, we need to encourage our relatives and approve the good things we see in one another.

While in your secret place, ask Creator Yahweh to show you your loved ones the way he sees them, for he sees the heart. Then you will be ready to fight for them the same way Creator Yahweh gave his life for you, laying down all to overcome the evil one. This takes great faith, but remember, your faith is in his mighty hand.

Eagle People...Today's reading is Hebrews 10:23-25.
Pleya gi. "Go with Blessings."

March 28

Pick up Your Shield

Every warrior has a creed he or she stands upon. There is something we are fighting for and something we are fighting against. Freedom is something worth fighting for. We can free our relatives and the ones we love from the power of the enemy. We fight for restoration of their souls. We fight against an enemy whose arrows pierce our hearts with doubt. This evil trickster has no power over us, unless we give it.

Now is the time to pick up your shield and protect yourself. This shield is the shield of faith that Creator Yahweh has given you.

Yes. It is a dreadful thing to fall into the hands of the Living God, our Great Chief and Captain, but not if you have received his Light and are holding onto his shield of faith. For once doing so, he is forever your Holy Father. Trust Him. He will complete the work he began in you and he will not be a moment too late.

Eagle People…Today's reading is Hebrews 10:26-31.
Pleya gi. "Go with Blessings."

March 29

Remember The Joy

Warrior, remember those earlier days after you received the Light, when you stood your ground in a great contest in the face of suffering. You felt strong then, invincible. You knew Spirit power was enough. You could face any enemy, no matter how great or strong or how many arrows they threw at you. You joyfully accepted the loss of all your earthly treasures, because you knew the supreme joy of real spiritual treasure that far surpasses all else. This newfound joy carried you through every sorrow.

Remember that joy now while you are still in the secret place on the Sacred Mountain. Cling to it as a treasure you never want to lose. This will help you to stand strong when insults are hurled your way, and this joy will help equip you with all the things a true warrior needs to protect the ones he loves.

Do not throw away your confidence! What Creator Yahweh has promised he will do. Do not be of those who shrink back and are destroyed but instead join the joyful assembly of fellow warriors who believe and are saved. Yahweh. Yahweh. Yahweh. He is forever faithful.

Eagle People…Today's reading is Hebrews 10:32-39.
Pleya gi. "Go with Blessings."

March 30

Listen Carefully

Eagle People, while still in your secret place on the Sacred Mountain (whether physical or in the Spirit) take a few moments to remember this one we call Creator Yahweh. Feel his sweet touch in the gentle breezes caressing each blade of grass.

See him in the morning sun as it rises and covers the earth with its warmth and light. Hear Him in the cry of a newborn baby taking its first breath of life. From the rising of the sun to the setting of the same, acknowledge his glory.

Put your hope in Creator Yahweh, the Maker of heaven and earth, the sea, and everything in them—our Great Chief and Captain, who remains faithful forever. He upholds the cause of the oppressed and gives food to the hungry. He calls you by your secret name. Listen carefully to His voice.

Eagle People...Today's reading is Psalm 146.
Pleya gi. "Go with Blessings."

March 31

Be Still

Taamtgi, warrior, "be still." Creator Yahweh's righteousness covers you. Rest and read the *Sacred Writings* until his whispered voice washes through your mind and sinks deep into your heart, birthing hope where despair has taken hold. This battle you face is not an Indian battle, not one that was lost over a hundred years ago. This battle began back in Eden, back in the beginning of time when brother Adam and sister Eve made the first wrong choice.

This battle has already been won, two thousand years ago when Creator Yahweh took on flesh and conquered sin and death.

Let peace fall over you as you enter a world where all is made right. Ride beside your Great Chief and Captain, both of you mounted on winged horses, flying on the wind. The battle cry is called, but your scabbard is empty. The Sword is in the Captain's hand.

Eagle People...Today's reading is Jeremiah 15:11-21.
Pleya gi. "Go with Blessings."

Cobby Shadley
(Ghostdancer's brother)

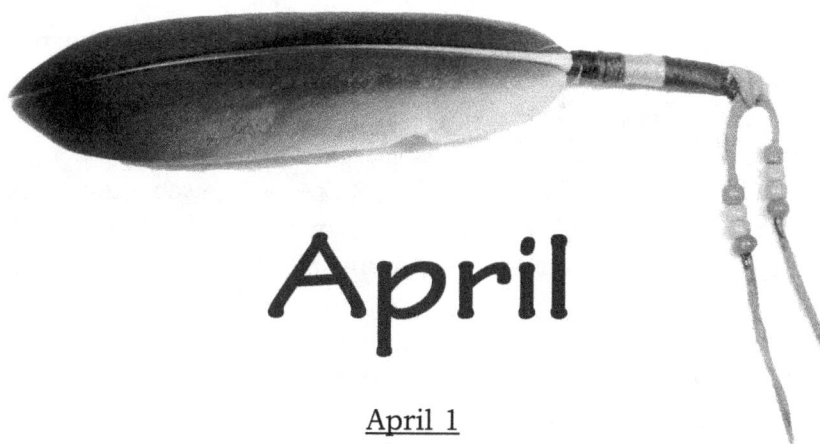

April

April 1

Hold Onto Your Courage

Warrior, fix your thoughts on Creator Yahweh. He is completely holy and shines brighter than the Sacred Mountain. His great Light brings life to those who live in deep darkness. He was faithful to the One who appointed him, even to death on a cross, and he was faithful as a Son to that One, The Most High God, the Great Spirit in whom we live and move and have our being.

Bear with me a little longer and I will show you that there is more to be said in Creator Yahweh's behalf. Do not long for the night. Beware of turning to evil. It is our tendency to love darkness more than light. Do not allow yourself to be dragged down that road. You are of the Light as Creator Yahweh is of the Light. The Light shines in the darkness, but the darkness has not understood it. Do not love darkness more than light. No good thing dwells there in the land of death. Hold on to your courage and the hope of which we boast. For he who said he would return, will return, at just the right time. Let him find you ready and waiting.

Eagle People...Today's reading is Hebrews 3:1-6.
Pleya gi. "Go with Blessings."

59

<u>April 2</u>

Our Great Chief & Captain

I will sing of the love of Creator Yahweh forever; with my songs and dance I will make His faithfulness known to all my children and grandchildren. I will declare that His love stands firm forever. His faithfulness is established and unshakable.

The heavens praise the wonders of Creator Yahweh, they speak of his faithfulness to all the holy ones. For who in the skies above can compare with our Great Chief and Captain? Who is like him among the heavenly beings?

Creator Yahweh is above all, beyond all, before all and in all. He rules over the surging sea. With one word He stills the mighty waves. With one swish of his strong arm he scatters his enemies. With one touch he calms the troubled soul. The heavens are his and swiftly answer his command. The earth is also his for he created the world and all that is in it.

It is good to trust in such a One as this. "Only be careful, and watch yourselves closely so that you do not forget the things your eyes have seen or let them slip from your heart as long as you live. Teach them to your children and to their children after them." Deuteronomy 4:9 (NIV)

Eagle People...Today's reading is Psalm 89:1-13.
Pleya gi. "Go with Blessings."

<u>April 3</u>

Ancient Days

A sk now about the ancient days, long before your time, when Creator Yahweh created humankind on the earth; ask from one end of the heavens to the other. Has anything so great as this ever happened, or has anything like it ever been heard of? Has any other people heard the voice of God speaking out of fire, as you have, and lived?

Our elders taught us well, to love and honor Creator above all, to honor the works of his hands as having been formed by him, and to treat each other with honor and respect. With honor and dignity Creator Yahweh led our people through the fires, and we have survived and come out stronger because of it.

Now, warrior, continue to love Creator Yahweh, Jesus Yeshua, with all your heart, soul, mind and strength. Acknowledge and take to heart this day that Creator Yahweh is God in heaven above and on the earth below. There is no other!

Eagle People...Today's reading is Deuteronomy 4:32-38.
Pleya gi. "Go with Blessings."

April 4

Creator Redeemer!

Join with the thousands upon thousands of flaming tongues that sing Creator Yahweh's praise! Our Creator has also become our Redeemer. He has bought us with his precious blood. There is no greater sacrifice than this.

Honor him with your most precious gift, your heart. Let him seal it with his blood. Let him lay claim to you as your Great Chief and Captain. Fall at his feet and become indebted to his great grace. Then rise and dance as never before! He has risen. Let the whole earth sing his praise!

Eagle People...Today's reading is Acts 1:1-11.
Pleya gi. "Go with Blessings."

April 5

Quick to Listen

My dear brothers and sisters, let us be quick to listen, slow to speak and slow to get angry. Anger can never make things right in Creator Yahweh's sight. So let us get rid of all the anger and moral filth in our lives, and humbly accept the message Creator Yahweh has planted in our hearts, for it is strong enough to save our souls.

It is true he has saved us from wrath through the power of his blood, but he has also given us his *Sacred Writings* (the *Bible*). And let us remember, it is a message to obey, not just to listen to.

If we don't obey we are only fooling ourselves. This is the way to live a life of true freedom.

Eagle People...Today's reading is James 1:19-27.
Pleya gi. "Go with Blessings."

April 6

Tossed by The Wind

Warrior, I know that you face many troubles in this land. Creator Yahweh told us this would happen for as long as we walk in the world. But he also promised that he would give us strength to break through to the other side. He walks with us on this path and he has gone before. He knows every step of the way.

If you lack wisdom on this, if you don't understand why he has allowed these troubles to touch your life, then ask Creator Yahweh for wisdom. But when you ask, you must believe and not doubt that he will give you this gift in his perfect time, otherwise you will doubt and be like a wave of the sea, blown and tossed by the wind.

Asking for wisdom does not mean that you will get the answer to all of your questions. But it does mean that you will receive a peace that passes your mind's understanding. This peace will help you to persevere under trial and lead you into the path of pure joy.

Eagle People...Today's reading is James 1:1-12.
Pleya gi. "Go with Blessings."

April 7

Magnificent One

Warriors, if Creator Yahweh came back today, would you see Him standing before you? When you lay on your bed at night, do you recognize his voice when he whispers in your ear? Or is your mind too busy, thinking about all the things you do day after day?

Do you recognize his smile in the sunrise across the Sacred Mountain? Do you know his touch when he heals you with his hand? Do you know his truth to free you from all your worldly gain? Or is your life too busy to take time to get close to the earth and be silent before the Magnificent One?

Day after day, Creator Yahweh does call, in a dream, in a vision in the night, through the reading of his *Sacred Writings*. In a whisper as gentle as a breeze. In a shout of thunder! He has spoken from the beginning of the world and he will continue to speak. He does not change like shifting shadows.

Eagle People...Today's reading is James 1:13-18.
Pleya gi. "Go with Blessings."

April 8

Make Ready!

Warrior, keep Creator Yahweh's decrees and commands, written in the *Sacred Writings (Bible)*, so that it may go well with you and your children for many generations and that you may live long in the land Creator Yahweh your God gives you for all time.

Remember how your Great Chief and Captain led you all the way through the dark times when you were imprisoned behind paper walls built by people who did not understand how much Creator Yahweh loves the way he designed you.

He was with you through those dark times, whispering his words of love in the wind blowing through the prairie grass and mountain forests. He called you along the singing brook. And inside concrete walls that held you captive, he was still there, bathing his wounded warriors in love. He fed you with every whispered word that fell from his mouth.

He calls you now. "Make ready, warriors, your time is soon to come." Eat the words of the *Sacred Writings* as if they are food for you that you cannot live without. They are the arrows that will fly against your enemy, and you will come out the victor in this war.

Eagle People...Today's reading is Deuteronomy 8:1-9.
Pleya gi. "Go with Blessings."

April 9

A Spiritual Battle

Hear me well, warriors. Our people have been oppressed far too long. The war cry has sounded! But we do not strike the battle cry against flesh and blood as we have done in the past. No! This is a spiritual battle that will affect everything in all worlds.

The ruler of the dark world is more clever and scheming than the trickster coyote, so make sure your breastplate of righteousness is in place, or you will go down in dishonor like a frightened rabbit that has wandered too far from its den.

This breastplate of righteousness contains integrity, moral honor and honesty and right standing with Creator Yahweh. It cannot be made with human hands and horn bones; it is made only through the blood of Jesus Yeshua. It is Creator Yahweh's protocol gift and cannot be bought.

If you have not already done so, ask Creator Yahweh for this gift of righteousness now. He will give it to you. And, though it will be large enough to cover you, it will not be too heavy. Its weight will be as nothing, allowing you to move freely in battle.

Eagle People...Today's reading is Isaiah 59:12-21.
Pleya gi. "Go with Blessings."

April 10

Hold Your Ground

Warriors, when your breastplate is in place, tighten your belt of Truth, which Creator Yahweh has given you through his *Sacred Writings.* Shod your feet with fine moccasins in preparation to face the enemy. Stand against the wicked one with the firm-footed stability, the promptness, and the readiness produced by the Gospel of peace.

Pick up your shield of saving faith that is able to quench all the flaming arrows of the wicked one, that evil trickster. And then take the helmet of salvation that Creator Yahweh, Jesus Yeshua has given you, and the sword that Holy Spirit wields, which is the *Sacred Writings,* the *Bible.* Now, you are ready to stand. Stand firm, therefore, and hold your ground.

Raise your voice and pray. Shout victory against the rulers and authorities of this dark world that will soon come to an end. Let the warrior's cry be heard throughout the land. Do not allow yourself to be distracted by the endless cares and troubles of this world. Such cares and troubles will soon pass away, but the Word and love of Creator Yahweh stand firm forever.

Eagle People...Today's reading is Ephesians 6:10-24.
Pleya gi. "Go with Blessings."

April 11

Flaming Arrows

Keep alert warriors! It is time to pick up our spears and flaming arrows. These flaming arrows are our prayers in the Spirit at all times for every reason and in every season. Pray and keep alert and watch carefully with perseverance as you intercede in behalf of all our people. With these prayers we make war against the powers of this present darkness. Powers that have held us captive for too long.

Pray that our chains will be released and freedom will be given so that we may proclaim boldly the mystery of the Good News of Creator Yahweh. Let us humble ourselves and come before him as ones who believe in the Great Chief above all.

Eagle People...Today's reading is Ephesians 6:18-24.
Pleya gi. "Go with Blessings."

April 12

Fleeing Shadows

No matter how far you go, dear warrior, no matter how deep the wrong. Whether the sun hangs high in the sky or deep blackness hides the light. Whether your heart is hard as cold winter ice or soft as the skin of a newborn lamb. Whether you run with horses or walk with shadows.

No matter who you hurt, or who has been hurt because of you, remember...not one drop of Jesus Yeshua's blood will ever be lessened. Creator Yahweh spilled his life for you and his arms are always open. One word from you and he will make the shadows fly away.

Eagle People...Today's reading is 1 John 1:1-4.
Pleya gi. "Go with Blessings."

April 13

Celebrate Your Uniqueness

Creator Yahweh designed you for a purpose that will soon come about. Honor Him and walk in his ways, for he is bringing you into a good land—a land whose streams teem with fish and pools of sweet water, with springs flowing in the valleys and hills; a land with plenty of food for you and your children; a land where you will lack nothing. Look at what is in your hand. Look at who you are, not at what someone else thinks you should be.

Look to Creator Yahweh for direction. You are a special design and as such have much to offer our world through the power of Holy Spirit. Celebrate your uniqueness.

Eagle People...Today's reading is Exodus 4:1-17.
Pleya gi. "Go with Blessings."

April 14

He Holds Nothing Back

Warriors, "who cuts a channel for the torrents of rain, and a path for the thunderstorm, to water a land where no man lives, a desert with no one in it, to satisfy a desolate wasteland and make it sprout with grass?" Job 38:25-27 (NIV)

How great is Creator Yahweh—beyond our understanding! He draws up the drops of water and fills the clouds with moisture, pouring abundant water on all creatures. When his voice resounds, he holds nothing back.

Creator Yahweh is our Great Chief and Captain. Is there anything he cannot do? Lay your life, with all of your concerns, sorrows, pain, dreams, visions and disappointments, in his hands. He is faithful beyond our understanding. Even when our hearts fail us for lack of faith, He remains faithful, for he has placed his Holy

Spirit in our hearts and he cannot disown himself. Trust him with your visions, he holds nothing back.

Eagle People...Today's reading is Job 38:1-11.
Pleya gi. "Go with Blessings."

April 15

Streams of Mercy

Are you thirsty warrior? Come to the streams of mercy at the feet of Creator Yahweh where the fountain of blessing never ceases. Drink and be filled and never thirst again. Jesus Yeshua sought you when you were far away, while you were lost and wandering on the dark path. He came to your rescue and bought you with his precious blood. Now fall to the earth and honor him as one who stands above all.

By his own mighty hand, Creator Yahweh, the one who designed you for a good purpose, has brought you to this place. By the same grace he will safely lead you home. Give him the gift of solitude. Give him the gift of silence. Let all else go and fix your thoughts on him. Let your wandering heart be still, and like a faithful dog soldier, stake yourself to his ground and remain steadfastly firm.

Eagle People...Today's reading is John 4:1-4.
Pleya gi. "Go with Blessings."

April 16

Orders to The Morning

Stand firm warriors! Keep walking the Beauty Way! Do not turn aside from hearing the truth or wander off into myths and man-made fictions. Do not chase mirages.

Our Great Chief and Captain, Creator Yahweh, gives orders to the morning and shows the dawn its place. He journeys to the springs of the sea and walks in the recesses of the deep. He knows the way to the abode of light and has entered the storehouses of the hail. Such a One is able to keep us from falling if we turn to him for truth. Do not waver from the truth.

Stand calm and steady, ready to accept every hardship without flinching. Keep the protocol and message alive. Perform all the works Creator Yahweh has assigned you.

Eagle People...Today's reading is Job 38:19-30.
Pleya gi. "Go with Blessings."

April 17

Finish The Journey Well

Standing firm will be difficult, warriors, impossible without the strength Holy Spirit gives, because many brothers and sisters will turn aside and not tolerate sacred instruction. Instead, they will chase after teachers and healers who satisfy the desires of their hearts for a season. But when trouble and calamity come, their souls will be empty and their courage will leave like a bird in flight.

Guard your hearts, warriors. Stand firm on the sacred truth. So when your time of crossing over arrives you will be able to say that you fought the good fight and finished the journey well, holding firmly to the faith Creator Yahweh placed in your heart.

Love Jesus Yeshua with all your heart, with all your soul, with all your mind and with all your strength. Long for his appearing like a bride on the eve of her wedding, for he will appear! And the time will be very soon.

Eagle People...Today's reading is 2 Timothy 4:1-8.
Pleya gi. "Go with Blessings."

April 18

Evil Lurks

Warriors, stop! Pull up your shield of faith. Evil lurks along the path, waiting to devour you. This is the enemy, that evil trickster, who often disguises himself as beauty.

This very real enemy wants to declare you unfit and unworthy of the prize Creator Yahweh has ordained for you. Do not listen to his lies. His tongue speaks death.

Do not take another step until you are sure of Creator Yahweh's direction. Read the *Sacred Writings* to avoid the trap the enemy has set for you this day, or you may fall into his pit and not even realize you have left the Good Way.

Eagle People...Today's reading is Galatians 3:1-14.
Pleya gi. "Go with Blessings."

April 19

Every Good & Perfect Gift

Warriors, we have died with Christ to the claims of the spiritual forces of this world, so let us not live as if we still belong to the dark path. Let us encourage our hearts with words of truth so we will not become disheartened. Creator Yahweh has called us to a unique task. We do not need anyone else to qualify us. Through his grace, he will give us every good and perfect gift needed to complete the journey.

When we called upon the name of Jesus Yeshua, Creator Yahweh filled us with his Spirit. Let us not set aside the grace of our Great Chief and Captain, for if righteousness could be gained through anything other than the cross, then Jesus Yeshua died for nothing.

Eagle People...Today's reading is John 19:28-37.
Pleya gi. "Go with Blessings."

April 20

Soul Sight

Warriors, work at loving one another. Do not let even a hint of bitterness take root in your heart. Take every unkind thought to Creator Yahweh, who knows the thoughts of all humans. Receive his gift of soul sight and see your relatives the way he sees them, as worthy of being loved and honored.

Approve the good you see in one another. Then, when the Day of Trouble comes you will be able to stand together, strong in the might of our Great Chief and Captain!

If someone truly is evil, then throw arrows of love at them; they will either come alongside you on the good way or they will receive the vengeance that only Creator Yahweh is able to give in true justice.

Pray for one another and share all good things. Give water to the thirsty and food to the hungry.

In this way you will make the path easier for your children to follow and it will go well with you and your children for many generations in the land Creator Yahweh your God gives you for all time. This is a promise he has given and he will not be late in its fulfillment.

Eagle People...Today's reading is Deuteronomy 4:39-40.
Pleya gi. "Go with Blessings."

April 21

Wisdom of Stillness

Warriors, is the way before you blocked? Are you hemmed in on every side? Stand firm. It is time to listen for Creator Yahweh's voice. Do not move until he reveals the way before you.

Do not listen to raven who will lead you into despair as he whispers evil words into your ear, telling you to give up and die. Coyote will trick you into cowardice and have you retreat into the world's ways of acting instead of fighting spiritual battles with all your passion. Crow will come with impatience crying, "Get up and do something!" Do not be tempted to listen to crow or you will miss the wisdom of stillness.

Stand firm! When owl comes with arrogance boasting that if you had real courage you would shout the battle cry and expect a miracle. Stand firm and wait. In times of uncertainty, listen to Holy Spirit. If you have any doubt, listen. If the way is blocked, listen. At just the right time, Creator Yahweh's voice will be as strong as falling water and as loud as thunder.

Eagle People...Today's reading is Job 37:1-5.
Pleya gi. "Go with Blessings."

April 22

Take Note of Wonder

Are you walking in the center of trouble? Take heart, warrior, Creator Yahweh is there! He is the one who saw you when your body was still unformed in your mother's womb. He called you by a special name even before you took your first breath in this world. He saw everything about you while you were being formed in that secret place, and he sees everything about you now as his Word is still at work in your life. You are still in the process of creation.

Instead of warring against the process, stop and take note of the wonder of what he is doing. Reflect on who you once were and rejoice that you are no longer the same. Let go of trusting in your own strength and wisdom. Spiritual forces cannot work if you are still trusting earthly forces.

Stand firm, and you will see the deliverance Creator Yahweh will soon bring. Remember that his main purpose is to bring many sons and daughters to glory, and you are now part of that glory.

Eagle People...Today's reading is Psalm 139:13-16.
Pleya gi. "Go with Blessings."

April 23

A Heartbeat Away

Warrior, do you know Creator Yahweh? Are you aware of his presence as something...someone...totally other? He is bigger, brighter, more all encompassing than you can imagine. We live and move and dance and become in him. He is both in me and I am in him. He's untouchable, yet He touches every part of me.

Feel the breath of his caress on your face. Breathe in the sweet scent of him, swim in the water of him. Let his sweetness quench your thirst. Bathe in the light of him and take comfort in the shadow of his wings. Let him be your every reason for existence, your hope, your joy, your tomorrow.

When you know Creator Yahweh in this way your life will never be the same. No pit will be so deep that he is not there. No sorrow so clenching that he cannot touch. No disappointment so shattering that he cannot mend and restore. Victory is a heartbeat away.

Eagle People...Today's reading is Psalm 118:1-13.
Pleya gi. "Go with Blessings."

April 24

The Word Spoken

L ong ago I had heard of Creator Yahweh, but not known the truth of him. No one can know the truth of him. Truth is as much a part of his being as soul and spirit are a part of mine. Truth is this person, this being that transcends every thought.

Pulsating with life, he is the word spoken, quickened in every beating heart. He is wisdom shouting in the street, love weeping in the night, an underlying refrain resonating inside every living soul.

Sing for the joy of such knowledge! Add your voice to thousands upon thousands of grateful creatures extolling and honoring our Great Chief and Captain through song! Yahweh. Yahweh. Yahweh.

Eagle People...Today's reading is Psalm 118:14-29.
Pleya gi. "Go with Blessings."

April 25

Captured by Joy!

A re you still weary, warrior? Does sorrow still rule your soul? Listen. A Native drum beats a tune older than the earth. Do you hear it? Listen again, tune your ears to the sounds of the earth.

Listen to coyote's song as it fills the night, the haunting call of loon as he welcomes the morning, the thrum of crow's wings in flight, but there is something deeper, a thrumming that underlies it all.

This thrumming is not a drumbeat after all; it is the heartbeat of Creator, thrumming across a vast expanse of sky. Breathe in the sweet fragrance of him and let him capture you with joy. Let laughter pour from your throat.

This is the One we serve! Creator Yahweh! The One who spoke the worlds into existence! The One who called your name before you were even born. Focus on him, and the weight of your sorrows will fall away.

Eagle People...Today's reading is Psalm 118:15-18.
Pleya gi. "Go with Blessings."

April 26

Day of Deliverance

Yes, warriors, we are sometimes sorrowful on this earthly journey, but don't allow your sorrow to cause you to become partners with those who reject Creator Yahweh. For even when our bodies walk the Sorrow Way, our souls rejoice!

We are poor, yet we often make many rich. We own nothing yet we possess everything. We endure troubles, hardships and distresses because of our devotion to our Great Chief and Captain. We honor him in hard work, sleepless nights and hunger; in purity, understanding, patience and kindness.

Like true dog soldiers we stay at our post in Holy Spirit power and sincere love; in truthful speech and in the power of Creator Yahweh; with weapons of righteousness in the right hand and in the left; through glory and dishonor, bad report and good report.

We can do all these things through Holy Spirit power, because we have been welcomed with grace as Creator Yahweh's people. Hang on, fellow warriors, now is the day of deliverance, first in the Spirit, but soon in the body. Open your hearts wide with love for your fellow warriors.

Eagle People...Today's reading is 2 Corinthians 6:1-13.
Pleya gi. "Go with Blessings."

April 27

Light of Heaven

Yes warriors, we are often misunderstood, even regarded as imposters, especially for our faith in Creator Yahweh. Yet we continue to carry the light of heaven in our souls. Creator Yahweh lives and walks among our people. He is our God and our Great Chief and Captain and there is none other like him. He has called us his sons and daughters and separated us as a people.

Since we are his children, fellow warriors, let us purify ourselves from everything that contaminates body and spirit. Let us set aside the ways of foreigners and begin the work of perfecting holiness out of reverence for Creator Yahweh. This is the way of walking in beauty.

Eagle People...Today's reading is 2 Corinthians 6:14-7:1.
Pleya gi. "Go with Blessings."

April 28

Take Flight

Warriors, it is possible that Creator Yahweh has allowed you to be chastened severely. If this is so, he will not give you over to death for he has conquered death, so that even if decay touches your body, it cannot touch your soul. Your soul is alive!

Let shouts of joy and victory resound in the camp! We will not die but live. Dance before Creator Yahweh! Let the bells on your feet match perfectly with Creator Yahweh's heartbeat. Wave your arms in a dance that is as much a part of you as the blood pumping through your veins. He made you for this very purpose. Give him honor through your traditions. Spread your arms wide, and in this realm of endless possibilities, let your soul suddenly take flight.

Eagle People...Today's reading is Psalm 118 19-20.
Pleya gi. "Go with Blessings."

April 29

A Unique Purpose

Do not lose heart, warrior. Yes, death is working its way through our bodies, sometimes through sickness or injury, sometimes in destroying our hopes and dreams, sometimes in broken relationships. But life is also at work, restoring our souls and recreating each of us for a unique purpose, a purpose designed by Creator Yahweh.

Jesus Yeshua rose from the dead, and he will also raise our bodies from the dead and present us perfect and faultless before his Father. He will also raise our dead hopes from the grave if we lay them at his feet as an offering of love. Sometimes he restores such dead hopes, other times he gives us something much better. At all times, we can trust in Holy Spirit power to guide us safely from the unknown and uncertain and into a sure hope.

Remember, Creator Yahweh is faithful even when we are faithless. Keep your heart focused on him. It is Holy Spirit power that keeps us walking the Beauty Way.

Eagle People...Today's reading is
2 Corinthians 4:13-16 & Isaiah 60:1-3.
Pleya gi. "Go with Blessings."

April 30

Life & Death

Dear warrior, what is on your mind? Words hold the power of life and death, not only spoken, but also written; not only written but also as thoughts. The enemy of our souls tries to rob us of good thoughts, filling our minds with words of death. Get close to the earth, sit in silence, open the *Sacred Writings* and let Holy Spirit speak words of life. Think of the goodness of Creator Yahweh. Think on what is true.

As the morning sun rises and pours new hope into our souls, think about Creator Yahweh's love for you. As the sun continues its walk across the sky and pours its warmth into every living thing, think about Jesus Yeshua and how he poured his life out for you. When the sun heads to its resting place in the west and you gather with your loved ones, think about how Creator Yahweh carried you through another day. When the sun disappears from the heavens and you stare at the star-filled sky, think about Creator Yahweh and how the splendor of his creation speaks truth day after day, night after night. There is no tongue or language where his voice is not heard.

All the glory and splendor you see in this world is temporary and fading away, but the love of Creator Yahweh endures forever.

Eagle People...Today's reading is Philippians 4:8.
Pleya gi. "Go with Blessings."

Don & Mary Gentry
(Ghostdancer's sister)

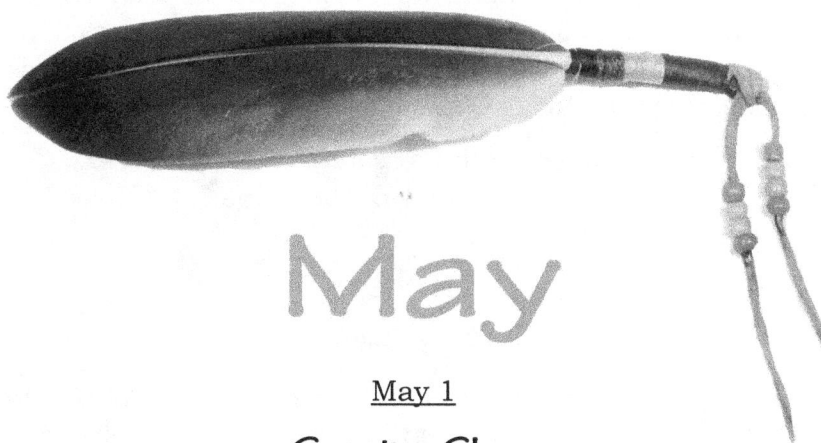

May

May 1

Greater Glory

Strengthen your courage, warriors! Our troubles and sorrows are also temporary and fading away. There is a greater beauty, a greater splendor, a greater glory that awaits us.

Time is short and our troubles are as nothing in comparison with the eternal purpose Creator Yahweh has designed for us. When put on the balance, the glory of our eternal purpose far outweighs all our sorrows and makes them light and momentary. Fix your eyes on what is unseen! Fix your eyes on Spirit! For everything we see with human eyes is temporary. What is unseen is eternal.

Eagle People...Today's reading is Psalm 118:19-20.
Pleya gi. "Go with Blessings."

May 2

Words of Kindness

Warriors, let us return to Creator Yahweh. Do not let your love and kindness waver as the night mist or the dew that goes early away. Let us honor our Great Chief and Captain with a steadfast goodness and love for him and for each other. Let us not neglect his words in the *Sacred Writings,* or we will become starving dogs picking at every scent of death, devouring each other at every whim and chance. Instead, let us eat the words of his *Sacred Writings* as if they are the only food that can save our souls!

77

Yes, we have been torn to pieces, but he will heal us; we have been injured, but he will bind up our wounds. He will revive us through the living water of the *Sacred Writings*. He will restore us with his own lifeblood that we may live in his presence. Speak words of kindness to one another. Walk in the Truth and Beauty Way.

Eagle People...Today's reading is Hosea 6:1-6.
Pleya gi. "Go with Blessings."

May 3

In The Camp

It is time, warriors, to seek Creator Yahweh. Do not give up until he comes and showers his gift of righteousness on you. Let us break up our uncultivated ground and inquire of him how he would have us live. Let seeds of righteousness take root and feed all who come near. Let us no longer eat the fruit of our lies or trust in our own strength or the strength of many warriors.

It is Creator Yahweh who taught us how to walk. He takes us in his arms and heals us. He has lifted the yoke from our necks and bends down to feed us with his Living Word.

Yes, warriors, we can live in his presence! Today, tomorrow, the rest of eternity. Let shouts of praise and joy rise from each of his unique children as we join in the dance with all of creation! Creator Yahweh is our God and we are his people. Let shouts of victory resound in the camp!

Eagle People...Today's reading is Hosea 10:12-11:4.
Pleya gi. "Go with Blessings."

May 4

Questions

Do you have questions warrior? Remember our brother Job in the *Sacred Writings* who faced a day worse than any we have ever known. One after another, his servants arrived to tell him of how he had lost his huge herd of oxen, sheep and camels. Then the worst news came that all of his children had died in a single day. In all these losses Job remained true in his devotion to Creator Yahweh. Not so, when Creator allowed the enemy to touch his body with terrible boils. Though Job never cursed God, he certainly had his questions.

What questions do you have? Yes, troubled warrior, we can take them to Creator Yahweh, but the better way, the way of blessing is to trust in Creator Yahweh's goodness. To believe in the deepest part of our souls that he is good and that he can bring good out of the worst of our troubles.

The enemy means these sorrows and troubles for our harm, but Creator Yahweh means them for good. This is a hard thing to trust in this way, but through Holy Spirit power we can accomplish it.

Eagle People...Today's reading is Job 38:31-41.
Pleya gi. "Go with Blessings."

May 5

Our Center

Remember, warriors, everything under heaven belongs to Creator Yahweh, and not only that, but his thoughts hold everything together. There is nothing too hard for him. Is there something you have given him that he should repay you? Of course not! For from him and through him and to him are all things.

Creation begins with him. Creation lives through him. Creation centers in him. Have you found your center in him? He has poured out mercy upon us. How unfathomable, how unsearchable are his judgments. His mystery is beyond our knowledge. Yet he calls us by name and we can dive into the depth of the riches and wisdom and knowledge of Creator Yahweh.

Shout to him with a loud voice and proclaim the magnificence of his goodness and character. Creator Yahweh is our God and there is no other! He alone can satisfy the deep hunger of our souls.

Eagle People...Today's reading is Romans 11:33-36.
Pleya gi. "Go with Blessings."

May 6

Like Those Who Dream

Yes, warriors, we had questions, but now our mouths are shut. We had heard of the wonders of Creator Yahweh, but like those who dream we woke to confusion and fear. Yet Creator Yahweh continues to number our days. Before a word is on our tongues, he knows it completely. He hunts the prey for the lioness. He counts the months till the doe bears her fawn. His thoughts of us outnumber the grains of the sand.

Take another look, warriors, and catch a glimpse of him, for just a glimpse is enough to hang our heads and say with our brother Job, "Oh, I didn't realize. I put a hand over my mouth. I spoke once, twice, but I will say no more. Surely I spoke of things I did not understand, things too wonderful for me to know." That is the truth of it, warriors, Creator Yahweh can do all things; no plan of his can be thwarted. Our Redeemer and Restorer lives! Our eyes will yet see him in all his glory! How my heart yearns within me.

Eagle People...Today's reading is Job 40:3 & 42:1-6.
Pleya gi. "Go with Blessings."

May 7

Paths of Promise

Don't forget, warriors, that there are many paths winding through a battle. Some paths lead to sorrow and destruction; other paths lead to heartache and ruin; some paths lead to the other side but at too great a cost. The path of prayer leads to victory where we either see the answer to the object of our prayers or faith fills our hearts with sight beyond what we see with our eyes.

This path of prayer is one of perseverance in intercession. We raise our petitions, and our hearts continue to cry out until Creator Yahweh gives us complete assurance. Then, and only then, it is okay to rest. Someone has said, "Wait at God's promise until he meets you there, for he always returns by the path of his promises." This is a good word for warriors traveling the path of prayer, because often the paths of prayer and promise are one and the same.

Follow the path of prayer until the promise is revealed.

Eagle People...Today's reading is
Luke 18:1-8 & 1 Thessalonians 5:17.
Pleya gi. "Go with Blessings."

Standing Tree

Courage, warriors! Together we are a standing tree that cannot be destroyed because of its fruit. Let all nations come and eat freely. In this way you will encourage your brothers and sisters and aunties and uncles and heap burning coals on the heads of your enemy.

In this present battle, you need no bow and arrow. Put away knife and spear. If your enemy is hungry, feed him. If he is thirsty, give him something to drink. As the *Sacred Writings* say, "If it is possible, as far as it depends on you, live at peace with everyone." To do this, you must keep a listening ear and a heart that is not quick to judge.

"Do not be overcome by evil, but overcome evil with good."

Eagle People...Today's reading is Romans 12:17-21.
Pleya gi. "Go with Blessings."

Sincere Love

Love must be sincere, warriors, loving first Creator Yahweh and then loving each other. Let us not love with words and tongue only, but with actions and in truth. As far as our enemies, let us bless those who persecute us. This is impossible in our own strength, but through Holy Spirit power we can do all things.

Let us mourn with those who mourn, raining our tears alongside theirs instead of giving a lecture on how to they can get past their sorrow. Instead, let us hold our tongues and weep with those who weep.

Conversely, when a brother or sister or auntie or uncle comes into a season of rejoicing, let us rejoice with them and dance with all our might. Let the truth of the *Sacred Writings* fill hungry souls as we walk the paths of promise and prayer.

Eagle People...Today's reading is Romans 12:5-8.
Pleya gi. "Go with Blessings."

May 10

Stronghold of Life

Has the way grown dark before you warriors? Do you feel yourself sinking into depression? Are the present circumstances that Creator Yahweh has allowed in your life sinking you into despair? Then it is time to stop, cease all work and be still.

Let Creator Yahweh be your refuge and stronghold of your life. Seek his face and inquire of him and do not move until he gives you direction. Rest in the arms of Creator Yahweh. It is a time to draw strength from a strong loved one and trust completely in another's strength. Wait for Jesus Yeshua and he will fill your heart with courage.

Eagle People...Today's reading is Psalm 27:1-4.
Pleya gi. "Go with Blessings."

May 11

In His Tent

Are you in trouble warrior? Cry aloud to Creator Yahweh. He will hear you and have mercy upon you and be gracious. Seek his face with all your heart and he will not hide his face from you. He will not forsake you, even if your father and mother forsake you and all your aunties and uncles. He will never cast you off for he is the God of your salvation.

In the day of trouble Creator Yahweh will hide you in his shelter. In the secret place of his tent he will hide you. He will set your feet high upon a rock. He will lift up your head above your enemies round about. And in his tent you will offer shouts of joy. You will sing, oh yes, you will sing!

Eagle People...Today's reading is Psalm 27:5-10.
Pleya gi. "Go with Blessings."

May 12

Born of Conflict

Warrior, are you still at rest in Creator Yahweh, hidden in the shelter of his tent? Do you realize that this rest is not born of open fields and wind swept skies but is born of conflict? Yes. The very thing that you looked at as bad has produced this fruit of peace. This peace is not like the calm before a storm so do not fear. This peace bears the quietness and freshness that follows the storm.

While you are here in this place of rest, learn the ways of Creator Yahweh and then when you rise to walk again, your feet will walk on straight paths. Even when others do not understand the way you travel, or when they bring false accusations against you, or even when some breathe violence against you, you need not fear. Wait for Creator Yahweh. He will strengthen your heart and give you courage, and at just the right time he will get your feet moving again.

Eagle People...Today's reading is Psalm 27:11-14.
Pleya gi. "Go with Blessings."

May 13

Carried to Safety

Creator Yahweh is our refuge and strength, an ever present help in trouble. Why do you fear, warrior? When trouble is near, Creator Yahweh is even nearer. If the earth gives way beneath your feet, he is still there. When the mountains fall into the heart of the sea, he is still there. When the waves roar and foam, and the mountains quake with their surging, Creator Yahweh is still there. He will catch you upon his wings and carry you to safety.

The wind howls, the earth rumbles, the shout of a horde of warriors rings out across the land! We hold our hands over our ears because of the noise of it, but Creator Yahweh is still there. Nations are in uproar! Kingdoms fall. Creator Yahweh is still there, carrying you upon his great wings.

Eagle People...Today's reading is Psalm 46:1-5.
Pleya gi. "Go with Blessings."

May 14

High Tower

Come and see the works of Creator Yahweh! He lifts his voice and the earth melts. He makes wars cease to the ends of the earth; he breaks the bow and shatters the spear, he burns the shields with fire.

There is a river, flowing feely forever, whose streams make glad the city of Creator Yahweh. This is the holy place for which our hearts long. Jesus Yeshua is in the midst of her and she will not be moved. The Great Chief of all the Angel Armies is with us! He is our Refuge, our Fortress, and our High Tower.

This is the one we serve! Our Great Chief and Captain! Be still before him and watch. He knows what he is doing and will accomplish all that is in his plan.

Eagle People...Today's reading is Psalm 46:6-11.
Pleya gi. "Go with Blessings."

May 15

Bow & Spear

Does it seem as if Creator Yahweh has hidden his face? Are you afraid he has forgotten your affliction and the taunts of those who oppress you?

Trust Creator Yahweh even in this. Do not turn from following the good way even when deep darkness covers the path. Do not forget the name of Creator Yahweh or that it is his hands that stretched out the heavens. He knows the secrets of the heart. Trust in the work he has done in the past and know that he will do it again.

We will tread upon the enemy who rises up against us. Do not trust in bow or spear, they will not save you. Trust only in the strength and faithfulness of Creator Yahweh.

Eagle People...Today's reading is Psalm 44.
Pleya gi. "Go with Blessings."

May 16

His Great Sword

Here is a good way of walking in beauty, trust in the Lord without wavering. Count on his righteousness to save you and know that it is not your mighty arm that will rescue you; it is his great Sword that will bring shouts of victory.

Let him examine your heart and mind. Make sure you do not sit with those who are false, and do not fellowship with pretenders. Hate the company of evildoers and do not sit long hours with the wicked or enjoy their ways.

Love the *Sacred Writings* and spend much time there in the presence of Creator Yahweh in the place where his glory dwells. Walk the way of integrity through Holy Spirit Power for he has redeemed and restored you, and has been merciful and gracious to you.

Eagle People...Today's reading is Psalm 26.
Pleya gi. "Go with Blessings."

May 17

A Double Portion

Warrior, when one enemy becomes two and two becomes twenty and help is still far away, lost in a place where you cannot touch her, wait for a double portion of Creator's Spirit. Bow your face to the ground and cover yourself with dust. Let your body cleave to the ground as one who belongs to it. For Creator Yahweh's sake we are killed all the day long; we are accounted as sheep for the slaughter. But do not let despair become your sister.

Creator Yahweh lives and rules in all dimensions. His Holy Spirit is able to touch and know every creature at each and every moment. Holy Spirit is not limited to time and space. His thoughts about you outnumber the grains of the sand. He alone knows your frame. Before you utter one word, He knows it completely. How can you not trust him?

Eagle People...Today's reading is 2 Samuel 22:1-11.
Pleya gi. "Go with Blessings."

May 18

Days Like Grass

Number your days rightly and you will gain a heart of wisdom, for our days are like grass, springing up in the morning when the sun pours life into us, but by evening we are dry and withered. What can we give to Creator Yahweh? What can we do that will make a difference to him? A thousand years in his sight are like a day that has just gone by, or like a watch in the night. With one sweep of his mighty hand our lives are wiped away and returned to dust. Yet he withholds that sweeping hand for a season and calls us by name and separates us to be his children forever; children born not of human desire but born of Spirit and water.

Creator Yahweh provides himself as our dwelling place and shelters us beneath his great wings. Before the mountains were born, he was there. Before he called forth the earth and the world, he was there. From everlasting to everlasting Creator Yahweh is God.

Eagle People...Today's reading is 2 Samuel 22:12-18.
Pleya gi. "Go with Blessings."

May 19

Spirit Talk

Warriors, there is a time, when your enemies are closing in behind you, that you must stop. This is a most difficult thing to do, because every fiber of your being will shout for you to move. This is a time to listen closely to Spirit talk; a time for needed rest and refreshment; a time to sharpen your tools and encourage your soul; a time to listen for Creator Yahweh's voice.

It is in times like these that stopping will actually haste your escape. Do not move until you hear Creator Yahweh's command. Then quickly do whatever he tells you to do. He will reach down from on high and take hold of you. He will draw you out of deep waters.

Eagle People...Today's reading is 2 Samuel 22:19-29.
Pleya gi. "Go with Blessings."

May 20

Run Through a Troop

When despair is your sister and sadness your brother, when hopeless are the parents who bore you. When they scream in your ears and taunt you with jibes, some honest and some untrue, but none with the scent of life; remember warrior, that to the faithful, Creator Yahweh reveals himself as faithful and to the blameless he shows himself as blameless.

We cannot be blameless in our own strength or effort, but Jesus Yeshua offers us the free gift of purity by giving his life in our place. It is his righteousness that protects us, his faithfulness that sustains us. At just the right time, Creator Yahweh will put wings on your feet and you will run through a troop. With your God you will leap over the walls that now seem insurmountable.

Eagle People...Today's reading is 2 Samuel 22:30-37.
Pleya gi. "Go with Blessings."

May 21

A Shield & Refuge

Warrior, do you know that Creator Yahweh takes delight in you? See! Even now, he rides upon the wings of the wind to come to your rescue. His voice thunders from heaven as he sends out arrows to scatter your enemies. He created you just as you are. He does not ask you to conform to another's idea of how you should walk. He has already set a path before you and equips you with everything you need to walk it.

Take joy in his delight over you. Break out in song when he delivers you from your enemy, from those who hated you, the ones who were too strong for you. He is your shield. Trust and take refuge in him.

Eagle People...Today's reading is 2 Samuel 22:38-43.
Pleya gi. "Go with Blessings."

May 22

Broaden The Pathway

Creator Yahweh is the lamp that turns our darkest hours into glorious light. His way is perfect and his word carries no flaw. He is the rock on which our feet stand. He arms us with strength and shows us how to walk in beauty. Whether leading through stormy, dark, forests of threatening wilderness or across wooded valleys teeming with life, his way is always perfect. For he takes what the enemy means for harm in our lives and uses it for good.

Who is Yahweh besides Creator? It is Creator Yahweh who arms us with strength and makes our way perfect. Let him broaden the pathway before us so that our ankles do not turn.

Eagle People...Today's reading is 2 Samuel 22:44-46.
Pleya gi. "Go with Blessings."

May 23

Dust Beneath Your Feet

Warrior, do not cower in fear when confronting your enemy. Creator Yahweh will gird you with strength so that you will pursue your enemies and crush them. You will beat them as fine dust beneath your feet. You will trample them like mud in the streets. For your enemies are not flesh and blood, but the principalities and powers of the dark world. They will lose heart and come trembling before you from their strongholds.

Creator Yahweh lives! Praise be to our Rock! Exalted be Creator, the Rock, our Savior! He is the God who avenges our people and sets us free from our enemies. Lift up shouts of joy and dance before our Great Chief and Captain who goes before us in battle.

Eagle People...Today's reading is 2 Samuel 22:47-51.
Pleya gi. "Go with Blessings."

The Eternal Spirit

There is no one like Creator Yahweh, who rides on the heavens to help you. See his majesty as he rides on the clouds in his glory! He is the Eternal Spirit, our refuge, and his everlasting arms hold us up. He will drive out our enemies before us, so we and our people will live in safety near falling water where the heavens drop dew. We will have no lack of any good thing.

Who is like us, a people saved by Jesus Yeshua? He is our shield and helper and our glorious sword. With a mighty bow and arrow he will scatter our enemies so that they cower before us, and we will trample them beneath our feet. Give praise to Creator Yahweh, our Great Chief and Captain. Yahweh. Yahweh. Yahweh. What he has promised he will make happen, and not a day too late.

Eagle People...Today's reading is
Deuteronomy 33:24-29.
Pleya gi. "Go with Blessings."

Beloved

May Creator Yahweh bless the land of our people with the "precious dew from heaven above and with the deep waters that lie below; with the best the sun brings forth and finest the moon can yield; with the choicest gifts of the ancient mountains and the fruitfulness of the everlasting hills; with the best gifts of the earth and its fullness and the favor of him who dwelt in the burning bush." Deuteronomy 33:13-16 (NIV)

Let all these rest on the head of our people as the beloved of Creator Yahweh who rests secure between his shoulders. Creator Yahweh shields us all day long.

Eagle People...Today's reading is
Deuteronomy 33:12-17.
Pleya gi. "Go with Blessings."

May 26

Truth in The Secret Place

Creator Yahweh always begins his work with broken hearts, people who will cry out to him for mercy according to his unfailing love; people who will call out upon his great compassion to blot out all their sin and wrong doings and cleanse them from all their evil ways.

Warriors, do not try to hide bloodguilt from Creator Yahweh. If you have done wrong, tell him so, for he desires truth in the secret places. If you ask, he will teach you truth in the inner rooms where no one else sees. Let him cleanse you with hyssop and sage so that you will be clean as falling water, let him wash you with his own blood so that you will be whiter than snow. This is a good way of beginning to walk in beauty.

Eagle People...Today's reading is Psalm 51:1-6.
Pleya gi. "Go with Blessings."

May 27

River of Sorrow

Warriors, before you offer the sweet smell of tobacco and sage, humble yourself before Creator Yahweh. Before you offer him the sacrifice of dancing your prayers, open your hearts before him. Let your hearts be broken with a river of sorrow because of the offenses we have committed against our Great Chief and Captain, for they are many. A broken and contrite heart he will not turn away.

Create in us a pure heart, O Creator Yahweh! Renew a steadfast spirit within our people and let us walk in the way of beauty. Do not cast our people away from your presence or take your Holy Spirit from us. Restore to us the joy of your salvation and renew a right spirit within our tribes and nations. Let our tongues sing of your righteousness. Open our lips to declare your glorious praise!

Eagle People...Today's reading is Psalm 51:7-19.
Pleya gi. "Go with Blessings."

May 28

Warriors of Integrity

Warriors, do you know what your life is about? What is worth fighting for? What forces compel you to act? What convictions mark you as a warrior of integrity?

In the *Sacred Writings*, Paul talks about being compelled by the Holy Spirit to go to Jerusalem. He admits that in every city the Holy Spirit warned him that prison and hardships and suffering were facing him, yet he still chose to go.

This is an amazing faith that is born of strong convictions and empowered through the Holy Spirit. He considered his life as nothing, but wanted only to finish the race and complete the task that Jesus Yeshua had assigned him—the task of testifying to the gospel of God's grace.

What task have you been assigned? What is in your hand? Take that task and that tool and charge with Holy Spirit power!

Eagle People...Today's reading is Acts 20:22-24.
Pleya gi. "Go with Blessings."

May 29

Such A Time As This

Warriors! This is a day to attempt great things for Creator Yahweh, but first we must take his faith in order to believe that we can do great things, and then we must take his strength in order to accomplish great things for him.

It is his work, not ours that will accomplish the task. It is his faith that encourages our hearts. It is his strength that keeps us going when all else falls away.

Let us be bold! Let us expect great things from Creator Yahweh! He is above all and through all and in all. He made the stars! And he has chosen us for just such a time as this and assigned each of us a unique task.

Together there is nothing that we cannot accomplish through him. With such a one as this it is easier to take hold of a lot than it is to take a little, so with arms open wide, let us take hold. But take heed, warriors, this taking is not for our own wishes but for the working of the task he has assigned us. The longer we walk the Jesus Way the more these two become one—his wishes become ours. Today, let us choose to walk in beauty.

Eagle People...Today's reading is Acts 20:25-27.
Pleya gi. "Go with Blessings."

May 30

A Tribal People

Creator Yahweh will not turn away a broken and contrite heart. Take care and be on guard for yourselves and the whole tribe over which the Holy Spirit has appointed you as a minister and guardian.

Look after the young ones and ignite the fire of hope in their hearts. Feed them with the *Sacred Writings* and return their hearts to their fathers.

Remind the fathers that Creator Yahweh bought them with his own blood. Warn them of the ferocious wolves that will get in among you and who will not spare the young and weak ones.

Be alert and on guard! Never stop night or day seriously admonishing and advising and exhorting each other with tears. We are a tribal people. We need each other. Do not believe the lies of the enemy that tell you otherwise. Love, even as Creator Yahweh loves us.

Eagle People ... Today's reading is Acts 20:28-31.
Pleya gi. "Go with Blessings."

May 31

Set Apart Ones

Warriors and children, Creator Yahweh will build you up! He has consecrated, purified and transformed your soul and he will give you your rightful inheritance among all God's set-apart ones.

I commit you to Creator Yahweh and give you to his charge, entrusting you to his protection and care. I commend you to the

Word of his grace and to the commands and counsels and promises of his unmerited favor.

Rest in his love. Live in his hope. Walk in his strength.

Eagle People...Today's reading is Acts 20:32-38.
Pleya gi. "Go with Blessings."

Aaron Gentry
(Ghostdancer's nephew)

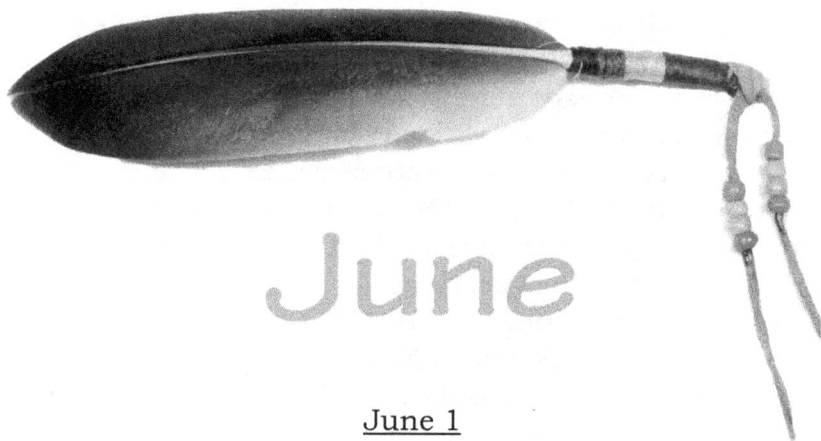

June

June 1

Marked with Blood

Warriors, there are ravenous wolves who lie in wait for your life. They are fierce and mighty men who band together against you, not for any sin you have embraced or fault that you have committed against them, but because you are marked with the blood of Creator Yahweh.

These wolves howl and snarl like dogs and go prowling among our dwelling places. Lies are on their lips, slander and ridicule belch out of their mouths. Do not listen to them. Pray to Creator Yahweh to deliver you from these bloodthirsty wolves and lift you above those who work evil, for they lie in wait for your life.

Creator Yahweh, the Great Chief of Angel Armies, will arise to come to your aid. Call upon him, wait for him, then watch and heed what he tells you. He is our strength and shield. He will bring down the ravenous wolves at just the right time.

Eagle People … Today's reading is Psalm 59:1-8.
Pleya gi. "Go with Blessings."

June 2

Steadfast Love

Watch and give heed warriors! Creator Yahweh is our strength and our shield. Dance your praises before him for his great mercy and steadfast love. He is our Great Chief, our defense and protector. He is a strong tower from which we observe with triumph the breaking down of our enemies.

Sing loud over the drum! Shout praises to Creator Yahweh for his great loving-kindness and mercy! Though many rise up against us, he is our great protector. He laughs in the face of our enemies and scoffs at their showing of strength. He shows no mercy to wicked traitors but showers his people with love. Let us sing of his strength and love. He is our great refuge in times of trouble. Yahweh. Yahweh. Yahweh. He is the God who shows us loving-kindness.

Eagle People...Today's reading is Psalm 59:9-10.
Pleya gi. "Go with Blessings."

June 3

Howling Prowlers

Take heed warriors! Creator Yahweh will not at this time slay our enemies completely lest we as a people forget the great things he has done for us. Our enemies will be trapped and taken in their pride for the cursing and lying they have uttered against us, but they will return at evening to howl and snarl like dogs as they go prowling among our tents.

Do not let their howling strike fear in your heart. Let them wander up and down for food and tarry all night. Their hunger for your blood will never be satisfied. Creator Yahweh is your strength and defense, your fortress and high tower. His mercy reaches far beyond our understanding. Watch for Creator Yahweh in the evening. Sing praise to him when the sun rises over the hill. Never cease from letting the praise of our Great Chief and Captain fall from your heart and lips.

Eagle People...Today's reading is Psalm 59:11-17.
Pleya gi. "Go with Blessings."

June 4

Pour Out Your Heart

Find rest my people, in Creator Yahweh alone. Your salvation comes only from him. He alone is your rock and your salvation; he is your fortress.

If you trust in him, you will never be shaken. When you feel as if you have been thrown to the earth in defeat, trust in Yahweh. When you feel like a leaning wall or a tottering fence, trust in him. When wicked people take delight in lies regarding your honor, pour out your heart to Creator Yahweh. Trust in his unfailing love.

Find rest for your soul in Creator Yahweh alone. Your hope comes only from him. Your salvation and your honor depend on him. He is your mighty Rock and Refuge. Pour out your heart to him. He will restore your soul.

Eagle People...Today's reading is Psalm 62:1-7.
Pleya gi. "Go with Blessings."

June 5

Rock of Unyielding Strength

Trust in Creator Yahweh at all times, oh my people. Get close to the earth and wait for him in silence. Let us pour out our hearts to him, for he is our refuge and strength. He is the rock that stands forever, even when all else falls. He is our defense and fortress.

Lowborn men are but a breath, the highborn are but a lie and delusion; if weighed on a balance, they are nothing; together they are only a breath. Riches are not something to set your heart on. Fame will fly with the wind. Possessions will steal your soul.

Set your hearts and minds on Creator Yahweh. Wait for him. His timing is perfect. Trust in him. He will not be a day late. He is stronger than the strongest warrior. He is more jealous than the jealous woman. He is our Rock of unyielding strength and impenetrable hardness. You belong to him. His love will reward you for keeping your trust in him. Lean on him, rely on him, and have confidence in Him at all times.

Eagle People...Today's reading is Psalm 62:8-12.
Pleya gi. "Go with Blessings."

June 6

All Relatives Near & Far

Warriors, stop! You were running a good race. Who cut in on you to keep you from obeying the truth? Creator Yahweh has given us two commands: to love him and to love others as we love ourselves. Are we picking and choosing who we wish to love? We are to love all our brothers, all our sisters, all our relatives near and far.

I see a sad thing beneath the light of the noonday sun. Creator Yahweh's people devour one another with their words. We look out for our own needs instead of trusting Creator Yahweh to meet every need. Do we have need of healed emotions? He will meet it. He may use a counselor to do so, but he should be our First Counselor. Are our bodies broken? He can meet that need too, and bring beauty even to the most broken of bodies. He may use a doctor to do so, but He should be our first Great Physician. Do we have need of justice? Oh, yes, we do. But there will be no true justice until He reigns supreme.

We are a spiritual people. We have always walked with one foot in both worlds. Let us return to our Great Chief with our whole hearts. Do not take another step until Creator Yahweh's love restores your broken soul. Then rise, and walk in beauty, and let love flow through every step.

Eagle People...Today's reading is Galatians 1:1-8.
Pleya gi. "Go with Blessings."

June 7

Words of Life

Love is often expressed in the words we speak. Are words of life coming out of our mouths? Are words of encouragement flowing among our people? Are we building one another up and thinking of others better than ourselves? Are our thoughts pleasing to our Creator Yahweh?

These are questions we must each ask ourselves every morning as the sun spills light on a new day. They are the same questions we ask ourselves when the sun is high in the sky and our mouths have poured forth a stream of words. At night when we lie on our beds we ask ourselves if we have spoken words of life or words of death.

Have our words pleased the One who made us? Have we been able to forgive in the same way he forgave us? This is a hard thing, but not impossible. All things are possible through Spirit power because of the blood of Jesus Yeshua who gave his life for us and covered us with his grace.

Eagle People...Today's reading is Romans 12:1-5.
Pleya gi. "Go with Blessings."

June 8

People of Grace

We are a people of grace! Our words should also be seasoned with grace. Who can you encourage on this day? Who have you torn down with words of death? Ask forgiveness. Speak words of love. Think on that which is lovely and good and true and just.

Yes. There is injustice, but Creator Yahweh will take care of that. We are not to take revenge. It is Creator Yahweh's right to avenge, and he will do it at just the right time, and not a day late. What if he had taken revenge on us before we gave our lives to him? Would justice have been served better? No! Perfect justice and perfect love met at the cross. Let us be a people who encourage one another with words of life.

Eagle People...Today's reading is 1 John 4:18-21.
Pleya gi. "Go with Blessings.

June 9

Overflowing Grace

Warriors, strengthen yourselves. Take courage! Do not go forward until you can go forward in the power of Creator Yahweh's love. Let victory come out of a life of overflowing grace. If you have not found this love; if you have not been cleansed with this grace, now is the time to do it. Seek Creator Yahweh with all your heart; with all your soul; with all your mind; and all your strength.

Do not let the sun go down on another day until you have fallen to the earth in humility. Ask him to reveal to you the darkness of the recesses of your soul. Then ask him to cleanse you with his shed blood that will make you as white as snow. Then dance, warriors, as you've never danced before, in victory and freedom! We cannot do this in our own power, but through Spirit Power we can do all things.

When we cannot find the source to love, to approve, to forgive, then we must go to Creator Yahweh and ask him to help us see as he sees...not with man's futile thinking that only sees the outside, but with our Great Chief's sight that pierces the hearts of all humans. Go in grace warriors. It is time to walk the Jesus Way.

Eagle People...Today's reading is 1 John 5:1-5.
Pleya gi. "Go with Blessings."

June 10

Footsteps

Creator Yahweh is our high tower. To him let us run! He is a fortress tall and strong. Creator Yahweh is a solid rock on which our feet can stand, and when our world is shaking, as it surely is, let us run to him.

His footsteps are everywhere. And they lead through dark places as well as through wind swept prairies. Keep your sight on him, and remember that the moment you receive anything from your Great Chief and Captain worth fighting for, your enemy comes seeking to devour and destroy.

Stand firm on the solid rock of Creator Yahweh. Power is developed through resistance.

Eagle People...Today's reading is 1 John 5:6-12.
Pleya gi. "Go with Blessings."

June 11

Deep Waters

Creator Yahweh is a shelter from the storm. He is a shade from the heat. He is a river that will never run dry. Run to him! And always find him near. He is the River flowing from the throne of God, whose streams make glad the City of Creator Yahweh, the Place where the Most High dwells.

The deep waters of Creator Yahweh's Spirit are always accessible, because they are always flowing. But first, you must leave the shore behind, and tread ankle deep, then knee deep. Do not look back! Tread on until the river takes you away. Do not be afraid, warriors, plunge beneath these waters. Though shocking and cold at first, they will become as a warm fathomless sea. The River of Creator Yahweh is your source of life-giving renewal.

Eagle People...Today's reading is 1 John 5:13-21.
Pleya gi. "Go with Blessings."

June 12

A Strong People

We are a strong people! No matter what fires we may be going through, let us honor Creator Yahweh with the praise of our lips. Let us shout out honor to his glorious name! He has been a stronghold for the poor, a shelter for the needy in our distress, a shade from the burning of the noonday sun.

In his time, and it will not be a day late, he will silence the uproar of foreigners and destroy the shroud of darkness that covers our people. He will swallow up death forever and wipe away every tear from our faces. He will remove the disgrace of his people from all the earth. Surely this is our Great Chief and Captain! We trust and hope in Creator Yahweh. He will yet save us. Let us rejoice and be glad in him. He will liberate us from the shackles that bind us and we will remain untouched by the flames. Dance before him warriors. He is worthy of all praise.

Eagle People...Today's reading is Isaiah 25.
Pleya gi. "Go with Blessings."

June 13

A Heart at Rest

Is your heart at rest warriors? I am not asking if you are busy or if your feet have stopped their pace. Your feet may be moving quite quickly and you may be in the heat of a great battle, but still your heart can be at rest. Creator Yahweh left us with his peace. His peace that was with him all the days he walked on this earth as Jesus Yeshua. This is the rest I talk of, the rest that brings great peace to a troubled soul.

Creator Yahweh's peace was there when the crowds followed him and would give him no physical rest. His peace was there when bloodthirsty men sought after his life. His peace was there when he stood before Pilate and proclaimed he was truth personified. His peace was there when he took all our wrongs upon himself and felt his own father had turned away from him, yet his heart still took courage. His peace was still there when he took his last breath.

Creator Yahweh's peace was there when he returned to his disciples and cooked fish for them over an open fire. His peace is still here among us through the power of his Spirit. His peace remains when all else fails and we are at an utter loss. His peace remains when all our loved ones fall away and we feel the pain of betrayal. His peace is the promise that will stay with us when we take our last breath. We know this peace when our ears are tuned to his voice, when his *Sacred Writings* become the food that feed our hungry souls, when we dive into his River and discover the source of Life.

Are you walking in Spirit power? Do you know his peace? Today, let our hearts be at rest as we continue to walk in beauty.

Eagle People...Today's reading is John 14:26-31.
Pleya gi. "Go with Blessings."

June 14

Singing Through The Storm

How merciful of Creator Yahweh to let us see what is in our hearts. If we did not see the anger boiling below the surface, we might think ourselves good. If we did not see the unkind thoughts, we might think ourselves kind. If we did not see the unrest and doubt, we might think ourselves just.

There is only One who is completely good and kind and just, and he knows the secret thoughts of our hearts. Yet, knowing them Creator Yahweh still calls us by name. His love sings across every storm that comes our way. Warriors, let us tune our ears and our hearts to his voice.

Eagle People...Today's reading is 1 John 1:5-10.
Pleya gi. "Go with Blessings."

June 15

Father to The Fatherless

Even in the darkest of stormy nights it is possible to break into a dance when you turn to the one who can heal your emotions and forgive all that is gone wrong and receive you as one of his children. Creator Yahweh is a Father to the fatherless and a Great Chief who will lead his people rightly.

Let us walk in his steps as he leads, growing stronger in his grace so that we can run with horses. With each step we will gain strength as we learn to love his law.

That great preacher, Ravi Zacharias, says that Creator Yahweh's law is worthy of our affection. "It was given for our good.," he says. "Let us learn to love his law. It is the most freeing thing when we understand it was made for our benefit."

We honor our Great Chief and Captain when we walk in obedience to his law. To walk in obedience is to love him and to love others. Are the secret thoughts of your heart honoring to him? Are you especially fond of his children? If not, let him cleanse you anew through the washing of Holy Spirit. If yes, then dance before him in complete freedom.

Eagle People...Today's reading is 1 John 2:1-7.
Pleya gi. "Go with Blessings."

June 16

A Great Prize!

Warriors, are you still wading through the waters of deep sorrow? Know this, although our enemy means this sorrow for your harm, Creator Yahweh will use it for good. Yes. Your heart may be toughened with deep scars, and sadness may take root in your soul. It is true that this sadness and sorrow will change us; that we will never completely recover from our grief, but we have a choice on the outcome once we get on the other side of the river of sorrow.

If we choose to endure this sorrow as warriors being honored for our great bravery, then joy will one day shine through our darkest clouds. Joy was the very reason Jesus Yeshua allowed himself to be crucified. He saw us! His prize! We were set before him and he did not lose heart. Take courage warriors. A great prize is set before us, though we see it but dimly while we walk this path of earth and fire.

Eagle People...Today's reading is Hebrews 12:1-11.
Pleya gi. "Go with Blessings."

June 17

Danger Waits!

Warriors, strengthen your feeble arms and weak knees! In order to walk the Beauty Way we must also walk in the way of love, and this way is often rocky and steep. Danger waits at every bend.

Take courage and make level paths for your feet. Clear the path so that the lame and young ones will be able to find their way behind you. To do this you must work at getting along with each other and loving Creator Yahweh.

Take the warm blanket of his generosity and let it fall over all our relatives and friends. Speak words of courage and strength to those of weak hearts. Let them know that Creator Yahweh will save them...and not a day too late.

Then shall the eyes of the blind be opened and the ears of the deaf shall be unstopped. Then shall the lame leap like a deer, and the tongue of the silent shall sing for joy. Falling waters shall break forth in the wilderness and streams in the desert. Yahweh. Yahweh. Yahweh. His great love strengthens the weary soul.

Eagle People...Today's reading is
Hebrews 12:12-13 & Isaiah 35:1-6.
Pleya gi. "Go with Blessings."

June 18

The Spiritual Realm

Warriors, make every effort, as far as it depends on you, to live at peace with all people, especially your relatives. Yes. You are a warrior, and you must be on your guard and fight the enemy with all of your strength.

But make no mistake in this, flesh and blood are not your enemies. Our battle is in the spiritual realm and our people have always walked with one foot in each realm. Walk in Holy Spirit power. See as Creator Yahweh sees. Hoards of evil spirits are gathering for the final battle. Be mindful of this in your skirmishes and strengthen yourselves in Creator Yahweh's grace.

Don't allow anyone to miss the grace of Creator Yahweh through a bitter root growing up and causing trouble and defiling relationships. Is a single meal worth more than relationship? Are many meals? Are possessions?

Do you not hear the outcry rising from the land? We do not own; we share. Let us share the grace of Creator Yahweh and give as we have been given.

Eagle People...Today's reading is
Hebrews 12:14-17 & Isaiah 35:7-8.
Pleya gi. "Go with Blessings."

June 19

Place of Refreshment

Warriors have you been swept away by Creator Yahweh's love? Like prayers being lifted up on eagle wings, sometimes even the toughest of warriors must be carried in Creator's arms, lifted high above the battle to a place of refreshment.

If this is where you find yourself, then rest and enjoy. Let the warmth of the morning sun wash over you in healing waves. Bask in the light of the *Sacred Writings,* and let Creator's words feed your weary soul. Get close to the earth and listen to His heartbeat. Count the rhythms of pulsating life in every creature you see. Climb to a high mountain and count the stars at night. Can you number them? This is the handiwork of his hands, and so are you.

Each thought that travels through your mind is held in his memory. Before the worlds began, you were in his thoughts, and he has held you there, and now his thoughts regarding you outnumber the grains of sand. He knows every choice you will make before you make it, yet he still chose you. He knows the outcome of every choice you might have taken. He sees behind and before. Rest in him, warriors. Let the sweet wind of his breath strike life into your innermost soul.

Eagle People...Today's reading is
Hebrews 12:18-24 & Isaiah 35:9-10.
Pleya gi. "Go with Blessings."

June 20

Bruised & Broken

Warriors, are you bruised and broken? Do not look at this trial as though something strange is happening. Strong and courageous warriors who have gone before us were also bruised and broken. The things we enjoy most today came about because they persevered through their struggle and sorrow.

This is where great heroes are born, in trouble, distress, heartache and adversity. Such things challenge us to persevere and to become more than we thought we could be, to become everything

Creator Yahweh created us to be. Every great hero has suffered great loss.

This adversity is merely part of that great shaking of things that can be shaken so that what remains is strong and true. We are a people who remain in spite of great adversity. Now, let us stand true.

Eagle People...Today's reading is Hebrews 12:25-29.
Pleya gi. "Go with Blessings."

June 21

Sacred Stillness

Warriors, this trouble you are going through may cause doubt and confusion to come into your life. The road of faith most often conflicts with caution and often leads through dangerous passes.

Well-meaning friends may encourage you to take the safe way when Creator Yahweh is leading you to something greater than what you or your friends can imagine.

At times like these it is important to quiet all the voices and sit in sacred stillness until you are aware of Creator Yahweh's presence. Search the *Sacred Writings* for guidance and focus on the One who knows every part of you. In this place of repentance and rest, you will find salvation, in quietness and trust, you will find courage and strength.

Eagle People...Today's reading is Isaiah 30:15-18.
Pleya gi. "Go with Blessings."

June 22

Spirit Gift

Warriors, are you still uncertain of which way to turn? Cry out to Creator Yahweh! Remain in his presence until you either receive a clear yes or a sure refusal.

To do this, you must climb the Sacred Mountain, whether physical or spiritual, and tune out any outside influence. Stay in your sacred place until Creator Yahweh's peace fills your every longing. Although you may eat the bread of adversity and drink the water of affliction, the time will come and not a day too late, when you will see your teachers with your own eyes. Wait for that time and you will receive the Spirit gift that will keep you walking in Beauty.

Eagle People...Today's reading is Isaiah 30:19-20. *Pleya gi.* "Go with Blessings."

June 23

Though The Fig Tree Does Not Bud

Warriors, there comes a time when everything around us is falling apart and yet we know in our hearts we must rejoice. To do otherwise would be like imitating that prophet, Jonah who ran from Creator Yahweh and ended up in despair. Running to Creator Yahweh is always the best choice.

When we run to Creator Yahweh, then we can say with the prophet, Habakkuk, "Though the fig tree does not bud and there are no grapes on the vines, though the olive crop fails and the fields produce no food, though there are no sheep in the pen and no cattle in the stalls, yet I will rejoice! Yes. I will rejoice! I will rejoice in the Lord my Savior. The Sovereign Lord is my strength. He makes my feet like the feet of a deer, he enables me to go on the heights." Habakkuk 3:17-19 (NIV)

Eagle People...Today's reading is Habakkuk 3:16-19. *Pleya gi.* "Go with Blessings."

June 24

This is The Way

Warriors, have you heard Creator Yahweh's voice saying, "This is the way, walk in it"? Do not take a step to the right or the left until you recognize his voice leading the way. Do not rely on horses; do not trust in bow and arrow. Trust only in Creator Yahweh.

Our Great Chief and Captain will one day reign in righteousness! Each man and woman will be like a shelter from the wind and a refuge from the storm, like streams in the desert and the shadow of a great rock in a thirsty land. At that time, the eyes of those who see will no longer be closed, and the ears of those who hear will listen. The mind of the rash will know and understand, and the stammering tongue will be fluent and clear.

Listen for his voice. It will be like music to your longing ears.

Eagle People...Today's reading is
Isaiah 30:21-22 & Isaiah 31-32:4.
Pleya gi. "Go with Blessings."

June 25

Broken Treaties

A sad thing is happening in the earth. The land mourns and wastes away. Brave men cry aloud in the streets; the envoys of peace weep bitterly. Fewer travelers walk the beauty way. Treaties are broken, their witnesses are despised, no one is respected. If it were not for our hope in Creator Yahweh we would waste away like wind-blown dust.

Creator Yahweh is exalted! He dwells above all. Soon he will fill the earth with justice and righteousness, and not a day too late. He is the sure foundation for our times, a rich store of salvation and wisdom and knowledge. Take heed warriors, the reverence of Creator Yahweh is the key to this treasure. Guard this reverence with wind and fire and never let it go.

Eagle People...Today's reading is Isaiah 33:1-9.
Pleya gi. "Go with Blessings."

June 26

Consuming Fire

W ho is like Creator Yahweh? His voice thunders and the people flee. When he rises, the nations scatter. Who of us can dwell with such a consuming fire? Except for his great love poured out through Jesus Yeshua on the cross, we would be like cut thorn bushes quickly set ablaze. There is no goodness that we can give him, no righteousness from our own storehouses, no treasure that he does not already own.

With a great shout, let our voices cry out to Creator Yahweh. "Great Chief and Captain be gracious to us! We long for you like a dry and thirsty land longs for water. Be our strength every morning, our hope at noonday, our salvation in time of distress."

Before a word is on our tongues, Creator Yahweh knows it completely. Deliverance is already on its way.

Eagle People...Today's reading is Isaiah 31-32:4.
Pleya gi. "Go with Blessings."

June 27

Sacred Writings

Warriors, do not neglect the *Sacred Writings* for they contain life for your soul! The Bible is Creator Yahweh's living words to you personally. It is also good for direction, correction, and protection and much more. It is the bow with which we send our flaming arrows into the enemy's heart. Remember that no spiritual battle is won without it.

Hide Creator Yahweh's words in your heart. Memorize them and have them ready as a weapon when the enemy attacks. Speak of them to your friends and relations. Whisper them while walking sacred paths through wild lands. Rejoice in the hope they offer you. Dive into the water of them and come out clean and refreshed. Let them be your guide and compass. In so doing, you will gain the strength and courage needed to continue walking in Beauty.

Eagle People...Today's reading is Hebrews 4:12-13.
Pleya gi. "Go with Blessings."

June 28

Redemption!

Look up warriors! Your redemption is drawing near. Whether it arrives in one hour or one year or a lifetime, it will not be a day late. Your eyes will see the Great Chief and Captain in his beauty and view a land that stretches far into the distance. The former terror will be nothing but a memory lost in the past. You will ask yourself,

"Where is that great chief? Where is the one who took our treasures? Where are the ones who counted the number of our people?"

You will see these arrogant people no more, those people of an obscure speech, with their strange, incomprehensible language. Your eyes will behold Creator's city, a peaceful abode, a tent that will not be moved; its stakes will never be pulled up, nor any of its ropes broken. There, Creator Yahweh will be our Mighty Chief. It will be like a place of broad flowing rivers and streams.

This is the city of our Great Chief and Captain, the place where many tongues and nations will dwell together in perfect unity, each person a celebration of the work of Creator Yahweh's hands. Creator Yahweh is our Great Chief and Captain; wait patiently for him; it is he who will save us.

Eagle People...Today's reading is Isaiah 33:17-22.
Pleya gi. "Go with Blessings."

June 29

Desert Trails

Creator Yahweh does not train his warriors in tents of ease and luxury. Do not be surprised if you find yourself crawling through muddy paths or across long desert trails that stretch far into the distance. Stark mountain paths are often the place of great testing, and deep waters reveal deeper faith.

Do not look at these trials as though something strange is happening to you. It is an honor to be counted worthy of testing by our Great Chief and Captain. He has an inheritance waiting for you. You have been given a new birth into a living hope through the resurrection of Jesus Yeshua from the dead.

This inheritance is a sure thing. Do not shrink from the fires that will refine your faith. Give great honor to our Great Chief and Captain, the Lover of our souls.

Eagle People...Today's reading is 1 Peter 1:1-9.
Pleya gi. "Go with Blessings."

June 30

Strangers in This World

Warriors be alert! Prepare your hearts and minds for action. The enemy attacks in many different ways. Do not allow yourself to be dragged back into those evil desires in which you used to walk. Those things have pleasure for a short time, but you are smarter than that now. Stop living for an emotional fix. Instead, fix your mind on our Great Chief and Captain and on his son Jesus Yeshua and do not conform any longer to the ways of the world.

We used to walk in those ways, but now we live as strangers in this world. We have been redeemed from the empty way of life whose desires are never satisfied. We have been purchased with the blood of Jesus Yeshua.

In this life journey we must pay careful attention to maintaining a deep consciousness of Creator Yahweh. Speak his name when you rise in the morning, think of him often as you travel through the day, and breathe in the sweet scent of him when you lie on your beds at night. Remember to speak of the good things he has done and set your hearts on his promises. By doing so you will not return to the empty life you once lived and you will continue to walk in Beauty.

Eagle People...Today's reading is 1 Peter 1:10-25.
Pleya gi. "Go with Blessings."

Frank Summers

July

July 1

Living Stones!

Warriors it is time to grow in our salvation and training, by soaking ourselves in the water of the *Sacred Writings* and ridding ourselves of everything that divides—depravity, deceit, insincerity, pretense, hypocrisy, grudges, envy, jealousy, slander and speaking evil about one another. These things are not becoming of our people and belong to our enemy. Do not be enticed by the lying tongue of that evil trickster.

We are living stones! Let grace abound so that we can be built into a spiritual house for a holy, consecrated priesthood. Let us build one another up and encourage one another in the gifts Creator Yahweh has given us. For we are a chosen race, a royal priesthood, a set-apart nation, purchased with Jesus Yeshua's blood and called out of darkness into his glorious light.

Eagle People...Today's reading is 1 Peter 2:1-9.
Pleya gi. "Go with Blessings."

July 2

Soar Above

Warriors, let us be eagle people! People who soar above the cares and concerns of the ordinary and wage battle in the spiritual world. May our vision remain sharp and clean and let us crave pure spiritual milk from the *Sacred Writings*. Let us dive into the *Sacred Writings* so that the truth of them will completely consume our thoughts. Let us weigh everything by this truth that passes all understanding.

Use the *Sacred Writings* to encourage one another, to stir up each other's gifts, to weigh truth, to correct and to confirm. Then, when it is time to do battle, take the *Sacred Writings* as flaming arrows and make sure your aim is swift and true.

Eagle People...Today's reading is 1 Peter 2:10-17.
Pleya gi. "Go with Blessings."

July 3

Free People

Let us live as free people! As servants of Creator Yahweh. For it is his will and intention that by doing right we will silence the ignorant charges and ill-informed criticisms of foolish persons. So let us show honor and respect to one another and love each other. Let us also show honor and reverence to Creator Yahweh, our Great Chief and Captain.

Jesus Yeshua set the example for us. When insults were hurled at him, he remained silent. When he was abused and suffered great pain, he made no threats. He trusted it all to His Father who judges all things fairly. One day he will judge all things and his righteous judgment will not come a day too late. By his wounds we have been healed, let us receive his healing and walk forward in beauty.

Eagle People...Today's reading is 1 Peter 2:18-25.
Pleya gi. "Go with Blessings."

July 4

Words of Life

Warriors do you want to make a difference in this world? Keep walking the beauty way. Do what is right. Never return evil for evil. Don't scold or berate others. Instead, pray for those who anger and insult you. Pray blessing and happiness on these pitiful people. Yes, this is a difficult thing, but you are warriors!

You have been called to inherit a blessing from Creator Yahweh. Stay on the path and one day you will hear Creator Yahweh say, "Well done good and faithful servant."

But watch the tongue, for with it mighty fires have been started. And watch the words that pour out on the airwaves. Words hold the power of life and death, and written words are here for all to see. What do your cousins receive from you? Words of life? Or words of death?

Eagle People...Today's reading is 1 Peter 3:8-12.
Pleya gi. "Go with Blessings."

July 5

Not Forgotten

Take heart warriors! Do not become weary in well doing for at just the right time you will reap a bountiful harvest. Creator Yahweh has filled us with Spirit power and he hears our prayers. He can make the crooked paths straight and he can take the weakest of warriors, or even an entire nation, and pour out enough strength and wisdom and courage for each of us, as well as our nation, to make a mark in history that will not be forgotten.

Wait for Creator Yahweh. He will not be a moment too late.

Eagle People...Today's reading is 1 Peter 3:8-12.
Pleya gi. "Go with Blessings."

July 6

Broken People

Are you hanging your head warrior? Do you feel as if Creator Yahweh has forgotten you? That a river of pain has swept you in its firm grasp? Take heart. Keep your eyes on your Chief and Captain! There is no dark place where his grace does not sweep through with healing power. Even in this dark time he is still at work.

Yes. We are broken. Yes. We are wounded. Turn to Creator Yahweh. He is not looking for the strong, successful and victorious people. He fills broken people with Spirit power and uses them to rebuild the walls that have been torn down.

One day, and not a day too late, this pain will be forgotten, swept away in angel song.

Eagle People...Today's reading is 1 Peter 3:8-12.
Pleya gi. "Go with Blessings."

July 7

A Ready Answer

Always be ready to answer anyone who asks why you have such hope within you, but do it with kindness and respect, even when they mock and revile you. Yes, we will suffer, but it is better to suffer for doing right than to suffer for doing wrong. Jesus Yeshua suffered for us when we were walking a dark path.

Fix your eyes on Creator Yahweh. Let his love flow like a river, first ankle deep, then knee deep, then waste deep, then so deep you cannot walk in it. This love will carry you straight to Creator's heart.

Eagle People...Today's reading is 1 Peter 3:13-22.
Pleya gi. "Go with Blessings."

July 8

Run with Horses

No matter what you see with your eyes, remember that Creator Yahweh is always good and completely just. Do not be confused by the prosperity of wicked people or be amazed at the luxury they enjoy while you fear for your life. Do not fret that the name of Creator may be on their tongues while he is far from their hearts, for our Great Chief and Captain sees their hearts and he knows your needs.

Remember the great faithfulness and justice of Creator Yahweh. Hide his *Sacred Writings* in your heart and let his great promises become treasures to you. Never forget to praise him with sweet smelling sage and honor him with the drum.

If you have raced with men on foot and they have worn you out, how will you be ready to run with horses? And they are coming, warriors. The sound of their hooves will soon reach our ears.

Eagle People...Today's reading is Jeremiah 12:1-5.
Pleya gi. "Go with Blessings."

July 9

Both Worlds

As eagle people we walk with one foot in both worlds. One foot here, in the ordinary world taking note of needs and ways we can walk in Beauty, and another foot in the spiritual world where we wage war against the enemy of our souls. Be careful to pick your battles wisely and remember your Chief and Captain. Do not take one step without knowing his heart.

Creator Yahweh is Chief and Captain in both worlds! Keep your eyes fixed firmly on him and you will do exactly right. There is no enemy too powerful for him.

Eagle People...Today's reading is Jeremiah 15:19-21.
Pleya gi. "Go with Blessings."

July 10

Beautiful One!

Sing a new song to Creator Yahweh. Dance with all your might! The starry host rejoices and the earth is glad. The sea and all that is in it roars with the majesty of our Great Chief and Captain. Singing fields of wild grain lift their voice in praise of Creator. The forest is alive with the splendor of his Name. Eagles soar at the sound of his voice.

How can we do less than all of creation?

Let us praise his Holy Name. Let us bring glory and honor to him through loving each other and lifting up sweet praise to him on the drum and flute. Let us honor him with our obedience. Let us bring a favorable offering of tobacco or sage and come before him with trembling and reverence. Let our lives show forth his salvation day after day. Yahweh. Yahweh. Yahweh. Let us never forget this Beautiful One.

Eagle People...Today's reading is Psalm 96.
Pleya gi. "Go with Blessings."

July 11

Polished Arrows

Be careful warriors that no one deceives you and leads you into error, for it is possible to be led astray from walking in Beauty. Stand firm in your faith, but make sure your faith is based on real evidence provided in the *Sacred Writings*. By doing this you will be able to keep your heart free from trouble.

Yes. We have seen wars and heard rumors of war. We have seen nation rise against nation, and we have wept over earthquakes and famines throughout the world. Our own people have been mistreated and forgotten, and promises have been trampled underfoot. As bad as these things are, they are just the beginning of much worse to come.

Still, in such times as these, Creator Yahweh has told us to not let our hearts be troubled or frightened. He is still in control. Take courage warriors, we are like polished arrows kept in Creator Yahweh's quiver for just such a time as this.

Eagle People...Today's reading is Matthew 24:4-8.
Pleya gi. "Go with Blessings."

July 12

Ancient Paths

Take note warriors, nations are racing toward destruction, and men and women are running toward the great abyss. Repentance is the only way out of this dark path. Let us examine our hearts and test them, and let us return to Creator Yahweh with our whole hearts.

Stand at the crossroads and look! Test the ancient paths and see, ask where the Beauty Way is and walk in it, and you will find rest for your souls.

Let repentance rule in the hearts of our people as we beat the drum and lift up our hands to Creator Yahweh. Let our tears never cease in the watches of the night for the lives of our children. Do not lose hope warriors! Pour out your hearts to Creator Yahweh. He will not allow us to be cast off forever.

Eagle People...Today's reading is
Lamentations 2:18-19 & Jeremiah 6:16.
Pleya gi. "Go with Blessings."

July 13

Great Faithfulness

Creator Yahweh has poured out his great love upon us and redeemed us. His tender mercies never fail. Every morning, day after day, as the sun rises over the hill, his compassion shines forth and he fills us with himself. Then when the sun charts its way across the sky and finds rest in the mountains, his great faithfulness continues to sweep over us.

This is the sure hope we cling to. Let us dive into the river of his tender mercies. Let his love wash away the stain of the past. Bask in the wholeness of his being. Be still before him and know that he is above all. Humble yourself before him, for it is here you will find rest for your soul.

Eagle People...Today's reading is
Lamentations 3:19-23 & 40:42.
Pleya gi. "Go with Blessings."

July 14

Renewal

Creator Yahweh has seen the wrong done to us. He will uphold our cause! Call on his name, even from the depths of the darkest pit. He will hear our plea. He will not close his ears though it may sometimes seem as if he has covered himself with a dark cloud that no prayer will penetrate.

Let us send up prayers on eagle wings. They will be heard...and not a moment too late, even though sometimes it seems as if all is lost. Let us ask Creator Yahweh to turn us and restore us to himself. He will renew our days as of old.

Eagle People...Today's reading is Lamentations 3:46-47.
Pleya gi. "Go with Blessings."

July 15

Steadfast

The promise has been given! Joy will return to our hearts; our mourning will be turned into dancing! Creator Yahweh will himself restore us, making us strong, firm and steadfast.

Hang on! For your brothers and sisters throughout the entire world are undergoing the same kinds of suffering. But, after you have suffered a little while Creator Yahweh, the God of all grace, who has called you to his own eternal glory in Jesus Yeshua, will himself restore you, making you strong firm and steadfast!

But know this warriors, this "little while" is in Creator Yahweh's counting of time, not ours.

Eagle People...Today's reading is 1 Peter 5:10-11.
Pleya gi. "Go with Blessings."

July 16

Vigilance

Hang on warriors! Be vigilant and cautious at all times. Do not be surprised at the pain and suffering you are going through, Creator Yahweh said we would have trouble in this world. But he also said that he has overcome the world. Commit yourself to your faithful Creator and continue to do good.

Our enemy prowls the dark places like a roaring lion, seeking someone to seize upon and devour. Withstand him. Stand firm in your faith against his attack. Remain rooted, established, strong, immovable and determined.

You cannot do this on your own strength, but you can do it all through Spirit power.

Eagle People...Today's reading is 1 Peter 4:12-19.
Pleya gi. "Go with Blessings."

July 17

Righteous Judge

Creator Yahweh established the earth so that it cannot be moved. He is mightier than the mighty breakers and waves of the sea. He is more majestic than the mighty trees that reach toward heaven to praise his name. His works are marvelous among the nations. This Beautiful One will one day rule the people righteously and with justice, and He will judge the motives of our hearts with complete faithfulness and truth.

Is this not One we can trust with our lives? Is this not One we can depend on to lead us rightly? This is our Great Chief and Captain and Chief! We may not know where we are headed or what the outcome will be; it is simply enough to know that we walk this path with Creator Yahweh.

Eagle People...Today's reading is Psalm 95.
Pleya gi. "Go with Blessings."

July 18

Broken Promises

Is the journey different than what you first thought warrior? Is the path strewn with broken promises and unmet expectations? Be careful that you do not fall under the lie that Creator Yahweh has let you down. If he is the One who gave you the promise then it will be fulfilled, and not a day too late.

It is better to put your faith in the One who gave the promise than it is to believe in the promise itself. Sometimes our enemy, the trickster, has fooled us into thinking a promise has been given when in truth we have been trusting in the fulfillment of our own desires.

Trust in Creator Yahweh. He knows the deepest desires of your heart better than you do, and he is able to guard and keep that which has been entrusted to you from the beginning.

Eagle People...Today's reading is 2 Timothy 1:1-12.
Pleya gi. "Go with Blessings."

July 19

Precious Treasure

Hold fast warriors! Follow the teachings of Creator Yahweh found in the *Sacred Writings*. There is a good pattern here that is worth following. They will lead you to the Sacred Mountain, the Mountain of Vision Quests where you will find direction for what lies ahead. Guard the truth that you find there. It has been entrusted to you as a precious treasure.

You can do this by the power of Holy Spirit who makes his home in you.

Do not worry about others who refuse to follow. Pray that Creator Yahweh will grant them the same great mercy and kindness that he has granted you, that he will breathe on them his breath of fresh air so that they too will climb the Sacred Mountain and find life for their souls.

Eagle People...Today's reading is 2 Timothy 1:13-18.
Pleya gi. "Go with Blessings."

July 20

Winning The Battle

It is time warriors. Climb the Sacred Mountain, whether in Spirit or in the physical and catch a glimpse of The Beautiful One's face. Be strengthened in the grace that is only found in Jesus Yeshua. We all endure hardships as good warriors who are called to endure to the end of the battle.

No warrior who has enlisted in battle considers the daily needs of his existence. It is as if he has already died and thinks of nothing but winning the battle.

No one who has died to himself lives for himself. He is now living for others and thinking how he can preserve their lives. Keep your eyes on Creator Yahweh, our Great Chief and Captain!

Eagle People...Today's reading is 2 Timothy 2:1-11.
Pleya gi. "Go with Blessings."

July 21

Dog Soldiers

Stand your ground warriors! If we endure like good dog soldiers fighting to the end for our people, then we shall also reign with our Great Chief and Captain. But if we listen to the lies of our enemy, that great trickster, and we become discouraged to the point that we deny and disown and reject Creator Yahweh, then he will also deny and disown and reject us.

Yet, if we are faithless, he remains faithful because of his Word found in the *Sacred Writings* and because of his righteous character, for he cannot disown himself. He is always and completely faithful. A good warrior will strive to remain faithful to the ONE who remains faithful to his people. If we have died with him, we shall also live with him. Stake yourself into the solid ground of Creator Yahweh.

Eagle People...Today's reading is 2 Timothy 2:12-13.
Pleya gi. "Go with Blessings."

July 22

Created in Beauty

Be careful warriors what words come out of your mouth. Avoid tearing down each other, for it only tears down yourself when you do these things. Such talk undermines the faith of your brothers and sisters and causes them to stumble. Study the *Sacred Writings* and present yourself as one worthy of the title dog soldier. Let us be people who handle the *Sacred Writings* with respect and honor, skillfully teaching these truths to others.

Avoid all useless, idle talk, for it leads our people into more ungodliness and causes them to forget the great promises of Creator Yahweh who created us in beauty. This kind of talk will devour like a cancer and spread like gangrene throughout the whole tribe.

Instead, let us walk in the way of beauty and encourage one another with words that bring life to those who hear. In so doing, we will also speak life into our own souls.

Eagle People...Today's reading is 2 Timothy 2:14-18.
Pleya gi. "Go with Blessings."

July 23

Consecrated

Warriors, speak the truth regarding Creator Yahweh. This truth is found in the *Sacred Writings*. Light the sage and cleanse yourself from whatever is unclean and separate yourself from contact with anything that will take you away from the truth of Creator Yahweh. In this way you will make yourself as a vessel set apart for honor, consecrated for holy purposes, fit and ready for the good work of a warrior.

Have nothing to do with youthful lusts. Flee from them! They will only take you down to the pit and make your life meaningless. Instead take steady aim at living in conformity to the will of our Great Chief and Captain. Take captive every thought and pursue faith, love and peace with all your brothers and sisters who call upon Creator Yahweh with a pure heart.

Eagle People…Today's reading is 2 Timothy 2:19-22.
Pleya gi. "Go with Blessings."

July 24

The Beauty Way

Be careful warriors. Shut your mind firm against anything to do with controversies over ill-informed questionings. These types of conversations only create strife and breed quarrels.

Strong warriors do not waste time on such contentious quarrels. Instead, we must call upon Holy Spirit strength and keep calm and speak in love as one skilled and willing to suffer wrong.

Whenever you correct another, do so as one who speaks the Truth of Creator Yahweh, with gentleness and respect and with much love and grace, so that your opponents will catch a glimpse of the true way of walking in Beauty and so that they will eventually come to their senses and escape out of the snare of our enemy, that great trickster, and realize that they have been held captive by that evil power. Then they will be ready to follow the way of Beauty and find life for their souls and you will have gained a brother or sister for eternity.

Eagle People...Today's reading is 2 Timothy 2:23-26.
Pleya gi. "Go with Blessings."

July 25

Lovers of Self

Know this! In the last days there will come great stress and trouble that will be most difficult to bear. People will no longer look at how they can love one another, but will be more concerned about how to love themselves. They will be concerned about storing up earthly treasures for themselves. They will be utterly self-centered, proud and arrogant, never diving into the *Sacred Writings* to find the truth for themselves but believing they already have the answers.

These people are not lovers of truth. They are proud and arrogant. They will no longer honor their grandfathers or show respect for the way of Beauty. They are ungrateful, unholy and profane.

These people are lovers of sensual pleasures and simple amusements more than lovers of Creator Yahweh. They choose walking in pleasure over walking in Beauty. They speak and carry a form of sacredness, but are in truth strangers to the power of genuine Holy Spirit power. They care more for being in the spotlight and having people talk about how spiritual they are.

Avoid these people! Do not let them drag you down into their way of thinking. Soak yourself in the *Sacred Writings* and continue to walk in Beauty, seeking to honor Creator Yahweh more than yourself.

Eagle People...Today's reading is 2 Timothy 3:1-5.
Pleya gi. "Go with Blessings."

July 26

Knowing Your Purpose

Be careful warriors. Don't be as one who will listen to anybody who will teach you. Pick your teachers wisely, making sure what they are teaching is in line with the *Sacred Writings*. Many speak with partial truth, even our enemy, that great trickster, does that! Study and know what is right. Avoid arguments that are always trying to get more information but never able to arrive at a recognition and knowledge of the Truth. These counterfeits should be rejected as far as the faith is concerned.

These people will put an end to themselves in due time. For their rashness and glory seeking will eventually become obvious. But you, warriors, should diligently continue to follow the Beauty Way, knowing your purpose in life, keeping your faith in Creator Yahweh with much patience, love, and steadfastness.

Eagle People...Today's reading is 2 Timothy 3:6-9.
Pleya gi. "Go with Blessings."

July 27

Equip Yourself

Warriors equip yourself for every good work by continuing to hold to the good things you have learned from the *Sacred Writings.* In this way you will gain the instruction and understanding needed to grow your faith.

This faith will lead you to absolute trust and confidence in the power, wisdom and goodness of Jesus Yeshua. Such confidence will give you the strength and courage necessary to live your life as warriors who protect and preserve our way of life.

Do not neglect the *Sacred Writings,* for every word is breathed by Creator Yahweh and holds instruction for the journey. It offers conviction when you have waivered from the right path, correction to get you back on course, and training in the way to live in conformity with Creator Yahweh's will in thought, purpose and action.

When your will has conformed to the will of Creator Yahweh you will better understand your unique standing within his creation, and you will become a light to your people that will lead them through the darkest night.

Eagle People...Today's reading is 2 Timothy 3:10-17.
Pleya gi. "Go with Blessings."

July 28

Our Hiding Place

Warriors, there is much to be said in Creator Yahweh's behalf. He has searched our hearts and considered our every thought. He knows when we sit beside still waters with bowed heads and when we soar on the heights with eagles. He searches our paths before and behind, knowing when we walk in beauty and when we walk in sorrow because of wrong choices. He knows the rain falls on the just and unjust alike and his compassion reaches out to fill our empty spaces.

He is acquainted with our grief and all our ways and has given us unique gifts with which to honor him. He knows when we hoard these gifts for ourselves and when we give generously. Before you speak one word, he knows it. He knows every choice you make and every choice you might have made. He has hidden you in the shadow of his wings and laid his hand upon you.

He is your shield on the right and your buckler on the left. Such a One as this, Creator Yahweh, is above and beyond our scope of understanding. We cannot comprehend how his thoughts hold us together or how we live and move and have our being in him while at the same time being filled with him. This One is not a man. This One is Spirit. Our Great Chief and Captain. Yet he became a man and opened the way for us to know him even as he knows us. Will you trust this One? Will you give him honor by turning to him each morning and bowing before him each night?

Eagle People…Today's reading is Psalm 139:1-6.
Pleya gi. "Go with Blessings."

July 29

Joy in The Camp!

If I rise on the wings of the morning and touch Creator Yahweh with my prayer, He is there. If I settle on the far side of the sea far from the land of my grandfathers, He is there. If I make my bed with the evil one, that clever trickster, Creator Yahweh is even there. The darkness is not dark enough to hide me. The light reveals every essence of my being. There is no place I can flee from his mighty presence.

He created the innermost parts of me, the soul that outlives this weary body. He created my body as well and formed me in my mother's womb. Creator Yahweh leads me by hand through every storm and upholds me with his righteous right hand.

Wonderful are the works of Creator Yahweh. My soul knows that full well. Let shouts of joy resound in the camp! Yahweh. Yahweh. Yahweh. How awesome is our Great Chief and Captain!

Eagle People...Today's reading is Psalm 139:7-14.
Pleya gi. "Go with Blessings."

July 30

In His Mind

Listen up warriors at the wonder of your birth! Creator Yahweh saw you when you were yet an unformed substance, hidden in the secret place. It was there in that region of darkness and mystery that he intricately embroidered the colors of your uniqueness. It was then He called you by name and in his book he wrote all the days of your life before even one took shape.

Before the world began you were in his mind. When he spoke the heavens into existence you were in his thoughts. He chose you to be his child, to be holy and blameless in his sight.

Dance before him warrior and celebrate his delight in you. Then offer him the sacrifice or a broken and contrite heart.

Eagle People...Today's reading is Psalm 139:15-16.
Pleya gi. "Go with Blessings."

July 31

Search Your Heart

Creator Yahweh's thoughts hold all things together. They outnumber the grains of all the world's sand. If he stopped thinking of you for one moment you would cease to exist. This is our Creator, the One who is aware of our every need.

Can you not trust him warrior?

Ask him to search your heart and see if there is anything in it that needs cleansing. Yes, our hearts are deceitful and we seldom realize just how deceitful they are. But Creator Yahweh is greater than our hearts and he knows everything. He does not give us the judgment we deserve, but instead he cleanses us with his own blood. Through Holy Spirit power we can walk in the way of Beauty and he will lead us into everlasting love.

Eagle People...Today's reading is Psalm 139:17-24.
Pleya gi. "Go with Blessings."

Ralph Medina

August

August 1

What Wonder!

Beat the drum and lift up praise to Creator Yahweh. He is our Rock and firm Strength. He teaches our hands to war and our fingers to fight all things that are evil.

He is our Steadfast Love, our Fortress, our High Tower and our Deliverer. Creator Yahweh is the Shield in Whom we trust and take refuge. He will subdue our enemies under us.

What wonder! What amazing love that this Great Chief and Captain takes notice of us, that he numbers the days of our lives and considers the hairs on our heads. We are but a breath or a shadow that quickly passes away, yet he calls us his children and gives unique gifts to us.

Praise his holy name and dance before him with joy!

Eagle People…Today's reading is Psalm 144:1-4.
Pleya gi. "Go with Blessings."

August 2

An Eternal Tribe

Warriors, do not put so much stock on earthly treasure. Do not fight over land or money or bloodlines. These things will all pass away. We have been bought with a price, the precious

133

blood of Jesus Yeshua. We belong to him and are all part of one tribe. We share our uniqueness with our earthly tribe, and it is a gift to be used for Creator Yahweh's glory, but our eternal tribe unites us as one. All else will pass away. But our position as children of Creator Yahweh will never pass away.

With these things in mind, store up for yourselves treasures in heaven, where moth and rust do not destroy and where thieves do not break in and steal. Consider that the only thing you can take into eternity with you is your loved ones, your aunties and uncles and cousins. Store these treasures in the well of Creator Yahweh's love, your greatest treasure of all. For where your treasure is, there your heart will be also.

Eagle People...Today's reading is Matthew 6:19-21.
Pleya gi. "Go with Blessings."

August 3

Where Your Treasure Is

Know this, warriors, your heart will tell you where your treasure is. It is where your mind strays when you are all alone. Most often it will stray to the things you've seen with your eyes. The eye is the lamp of the body. If your eye is sound, your entire body will be full of light and your thoughts will turn to the way of Beauty.

But if your eye is unsound, your whole body will be full of darkness. Be careful that you do not allow that darkness to overtake your thoughts, for you cannot serve two masters. Whatever holds your thoughts is your master. They are either Spirit thoughts or thoughts that drag you back into darkness.

Walk in the way of Beauty, be careful what you let your eyes see; soak yourself in the *Sacred Writings,* and set your heart on Creator Yahweh. By doing these things you will become a light for others to follow.

Eagle People...Today's reading is Matthew 6:22-24.
Pleya gi. "Go with Blessings."

August 4

Birds of The Air

Warriors, have you noticed the birds of the air? Eagle soars on the heights becoming one with the wind. The storms of life do not bother him. Osprey flies thousands of miles at just the right time, knowing full well his needs will be met. Hawk does not reap or sow or gather into barns; he hunts for food that he knows will be there. You, who are made in the image of Creator Yahweh, are more valuable than Eagle and Osprey and Hawk, though they are valuable as well.

Creator Yahweh is very much in touch with his creation. He will care for you. He watches when the doe bears her fawn. He counts the months till she gives birth. Her young thrive and grow strong in the wilds.

Creator Yahweh also sees your deepest need. He knows the empty spaces of your heart. So do everything you can to stop being anxious, because your worry cannot add one day to your life. Sing and dance your prayers to him and thank him that he cares for you.

Eagle People...Today's reading is
Matthew 6:25-27 & Job 39:1-4.
Pleya gi. "Go with Blessings."

August 5

Fields of Green

Warriors, do not worry about how you will clothe yourself, or what you will eat or drink. Everyone who does not believe in Creator Yahweh worries about these things. But you know that Creator Yahweh clothes the flowers with glorious colors and paints the grass with magnificent hues.

If he so clothes the grass of the field which today is alive and green and tomorrow is tossed into the furnace, then you know he will clothe you as well, you who are made in his image.

Creator Yahweh knows your needs. Trust him to take care of them at just the right time.

Eagle People...Today's reading is Matthew 6:28-33.
Pleya gi. "Go with Blessings."

August 6

Soaring Eagles

Keep on the path of walking in Beauty! Strive above all to bring Creator's beauty into this world through loving him and loving others. By doing this you will receive everything you need and much more. Do not even consider worrying about tomorrow, because you know today has enough troubles to rob your peace.

Creator Yahweh gave the horse his strength and clothes his neck with a flowing mane. Hawk takes flight by Creator Yahweh's wisdom and spreads his wings toward the south. Eagle soars at his command. Focus on serving your Chief and Captain well, as a faithful warrior like hawk and eagle, soaring to the heights of his love.

Eagle People...Today's reading is
Matthew 6:33-34 & Job 39:19-30.
Pleya gi. "Go with Blessings."

August 7

Spirit Power

Light the sage and come before Creator Yahweh with your requests. If you are walking in Holy Spirit power your requests will be in line with his desires for you.

Keep on asking and you will receive. Keep on seeking and you will find. Keep on knocking with reverence and the door will be opened.

For everyone who keeps on asking from a heart cleansed through the blood of Jesus Yeshua will receive; and anyone who keeps on seeking diligently will find the object of their hearts desire; and whoever keeps on knocking at the door Creator Yahweh has set before them will find the door opened. Let all else fall away as you continue to walk in the way of Beauty.

Eagle People...Today's reading is Matthew 7:1-11.
Pleya gi. "Go with Blessings."

August 8

Child For Eternity

Can you raise your voice to the clouds and cover yourself with a flood of Water? Do you send the lightning bolts on their way? Do you have the wisdom to count the clouds and can you tip over the water jars of the heavens? Our Great Chief and Captain does all these things and holds your days and nights in his hands.

He knew your beginning before you ever came to be. He knows your ending in this place we call time. He has called you to be his child for eternity. Trust your Great Chief and Captain warrior. He will provide your deepest needs and fulfill your heart's desires at just the right time.

Eagle People...Today's reading is Job 38:34-38.
Pleya gi. "Go with Blessings."

August 9

Armed With Strength

Warriors, be careful to not put too much hope in your own strength. It is Creator Yahweh who arms us with strength and makes our paths straight. He has been gracious to forgive his people for the pride of turning away from him. He has become our salvation and has caused his loving kindness and unfailing love to shower down upon us. At just the right time, he will revive and restore us!

Let us rejoice in Creator Yahweh with all our hearts and let us listen carefully to what he has to say in the *Sacred Writings*. He promises peace to his people, the ones who have accepted the covering of Jesus Yeshua's blood. Let us walk in that peace and never return to the pride of our self-arrogant folly.

Eagle People...Today's reading is Psalm 85:1-8.
Pleya gi. "Go with Blessings."

August 10

Faithful Warriors

Creator Yahweh's peace and glory will once again dwell in our land. We know this because he has given the promise and because love and faithfulness met together at the cross along with righteousness and peace. Let us rejoice and be glad! Let faithfulness spring forth from our hearts and truth from the earth.

Know this, warriors, righteousness goes before our Great Chief and Captain and prepares the way for his steps. Our land will once again yield its bountiful harvest. Hold tight to these promises, and let us be faithful warriors as we continue to walk in the Beauty way.

Eagle People...Today's reading is Psalm 85:9-13.
Pleya gi. "Go with Blessings."

August 11

Dancing Our Prayers

How lovely is the dwelling place of Creator Yahweh our Lord Almighty! My soul yearns and groans; for the courts of my Great Chief and Captain, yet his Spirit dwells inside my very soul. My heart and my flesh cry out and sing for joy to the Living God! Even the sparrow has found a home, and the swallow a nest for herself where she may have her young in safety close to the altar of Creator Yahweh. How happy, fortunate, and to be envied are all who dwell in the presence of Creator Yahweh. Let us dance our prayers before him knowing he cares for his people and loves us with an everlasting love.

Eagle People...Today's reading is Psalm 84:1-4.
Pleya gi. "Go with Blessings."

August 12

Falling Water

How happy, fortunate, and to be envied are all who find their strength in Creator Yahweh. This is the strength of a true warrior, one who has set his heart on following our great Chief

138

and Captain. When we pass through the valley of sorrows, they will become a place of unending springs, falling water that will cleanse and heal our people. We will go from strength to strength until the whole assembly of our people stands before our Great Leader.

Take note, warriors, when you have looked in all four directions and have failed to catch a glimpse of Creator Yahweh, he still sees and knows the way you take. Can you say that when he has tested you, you will come forth as gold; that your feet have closely followed his steps; that you have kept to his way without turning aside and have not departed from his commands?

Make it your goal to treasure the words of his mouth more than daily bread. This is the strength that will heal our people.

Eagle People...Today's reading is
Psalm 84:5-8 & Job 23:8-12.
Pleya gi. "Go with Blessings."

August 13

Our Shield & Sun!

Warriors, never forget that our Great Chief and Captain is our shield and sun! Those who look to him are radiant with his glory. Do not look to lesser things to receive your reward, for a day in his presence is better than a thousand anywhere else.

Be careful not to spend yourself for pleasure that lasts but a short season. It is better to be a doorkeeper in the house of Creator Yahweh than to dwell at ease and comfort in the tents of wickedness.

Creator bestows favor and honor on his faithful warriors and preserves every good thing for those who walk uprightly before him. How happy, fortunate, and to be envied are all who lean into our Great Chief and Captain. Let us commit our way to him and trust him with all confidence.

Eagle People...Today's reading is Psalm 84:9-12.
Pleya gi. "Go with Blessings."

August 14

The Strongest Dog Soldier

In the heat of the battle dog soldiers stake themselves to the ground and fight until the battle is either lost or won. They are like standing trees that have been torn apart and twisted by fierce winds, but these are the strongest of trees that stand long after the storm is spent.

Jesus Yeshua is the strongest Dog Soldier of all, placing himself between us and the fiercest of enemies.

Seek the faith of a dog soldier, for it is this faith that will carry you through the strongest spiritual storms. Faith grows during these storms.

Unbelief looks at Creator Yahweh through the circumstances of life that drag us down. But a dog soldier of faith looks at the circumstances through Jesus Yeshua knowing that Creator Yahweh will not allow the enemy to come too close. That evil trickster may break the body but he cannot break the soul.

Eagle People...Today's reading is Psalm 1.
Pleya gi. "Go with Blessings."

August 15

Mutual Encouragement

Be careful warriors, to welcome all our weaker brothers and sisters and cousins who love Creator Yahweh. Do not criticize their opinions, or pass judgment on their choices or perplex them with religious discussions. Such things are not part of walking the beauty way. It is not our place to judge the servants of our Great Chief and Captain. It is before Creator Yahweh that each of us will give an account of our own convictions and actions.

So let us no more criticize and blame and pass judgment on one another, but instead let us firmly decide and purpose to never put a stumbling block or any kind of hindrance in the way of a fellow warrior. Let us love one another as Creator Yahweh loves us and let us pursue what is good for soul harmony and for mutual encouragement of one another. This is a good way to walk in beauty.

Eagle People...Today's reading is Romans 14:1-19.
Pleya gi. "Go with Blessings."

August 16

Bear with Failings

Take note warriors, we who are strong ought to bear with the failings of our weak relatives and not just seek to please ourselves. Let us make it our goal to bring happiness to our neighbors for their good and welfare, to edify and strengthen them and to build them up spiritually. Jesus Yeshua set an example for us to follow in this matter, and the *Sacred Writings* encourage us in our steadfast endurance so that we can hold fast to the hope Creator has given us.

Together, with one voice and united hearts, let us praise and glorify our Great Chief and Captain and Father of our Lord Jesus Yeshua, the Messiah. Let us welcome and receive one another for the glory of Creator Yahweh.

Eagle People...Today's reading is Romans 14:20-15:6.
Pleya gi. "Go with Blessings."

August 17

Spirit People!

We are Spirit people! Because of the blood of Jesus Yeshua we can stand before Creator Yahweh completely clean and accepted. Not for anything we do, but because the law of the Spirit of life has freed us from the law of sin and death. This is a good reason to beat the drum and dance before our Great Chief and Captain!

Do not listen to the lies of our enemy, that evil trickster, who tells you that you are unworthy. Our Great Chief and Captain has done what the law could not do by sending his own Son in the form of a man so that the righteous and just requirement of the law might be fully met in us who live and move not in the ways of the flesh but in the ways of the Spirit.

Yes. We make mistakes. Yes we do wrong, but the flesh no longer controls us. Spirit power is now our master. Rebuke your enemy and stand in the glory of Creator Yahweh.

Eagle People...Today's reading is Romans 8:1-4.
Pleya gi. "Go with Blessings."

August 18

Eagle Power!

Creator Yahweh has instructed you, warriors, on how to walk in Beauty. Now I urge you to do so more and more. It is Creator's will that you should be holy; that you should avoid sexual immorality and that you should learn to control your own body in a way that is holy and honorable. Do not give in to passionate lust.

This is a difficult thing to do in your own strength, but you have been bought with a price! You no longer belong to the old way of thinking. You are now able to walk in Spirit power! Call upon Holy Spirit. Choose to deny yourself and follow Creator Yahweh. It is in losing ourselves that we discover the true freedom of Eagle power.

Eagle People...Today's reading is 1 Thessalonians 4:1-12.
Pleya gi. "Go with Blessings."

August 19

The Faith Way

Do you want a life of joy warriors! Then make it your ambition to love Creator Yahweh with all your heart, soul, mind and strength. Climb the Sacred Mountain (whether in Spirit or in the body) and discover Creator in the span of a far-seeing place. Hear his voice upon the wind singing through the trees, and recognize his touch when he heals you through Spirit power.

As you walk the Faith Way, thank Creator Yahweh for the many crossroads where you see his perfect leading, even in times of sorrow. As you see his love for you, you will be able to love others more and more. As you love others you will come to understand what a treasure you are to your Great Chief and Captain. In this way your joy will be made complete.

Eagle People...Today's reading is 1 John 1:1-4.
Pleya gi. "Go with Blessings."

August 20

Walk in The Light

Listen warriors, this is the message and promise our ancestors have heard from the beginning: Creator Yahweh is Light, and in him there is no darkness at all. If we claim to be faithful warriors of our Great Chief in Captain and we continue to walk in darkness, then we are not claiming the truth.

But if we walk in the Light as Creator is in the light, then we will have fellowship with one another, and the blood of Jesus Yeshua cleanses us from all guilt of wrong-doing. And the amazing thing is that he keeps us cleansed from all darkness in all its forms and manifestations.

Yahweh. Yahweh. Yahweh. All praise to our Creator Yahweh!

Eagle People...Today's reading is 1 John 1:5-7.
Pleya gi. "Go with Blessings."

August 21

A Cleansed Heart

Be careful warriors, if we say we have done no wrong, then we delude ourselves and lead ourselves astray and the Truth does not live in our hearts.

But if we freely admit that we have sinned and confess our wrong-doings, Creator Yahweh is faithful and true to his nature and his promises and will forgive our wrong doings and cleanse us from everything that is not in conformity to his will in purpose, thought, and action.

This is the ultimate action of walking the Beauty Way. A cleansed heart responds in joyful love!

Eagle People...Today's reading is 1 John 1:8-10.
Pleya gi. "Go with Blessings."

<u>August 22</u>

Perfecting Love

Fellow warriors, I have been writing to you about not walking in darkness so that we may not violate Creator Yahweh's commands. But if anyone does violate his commands, there is still hope! Jesus Yeshua will intercede and advocate for us so that his love is perfected in us.

This is the way of perfecting Creator Yahweh's love. Treasure his Word in the *Sacred Writings;* think often about his precepts, and obey his commands. By doing so the darkness will soon fall behind and you will walk steadily into glorious Light.

Creator Yahweh is clearing away the darkness and revealing himself to you. This is a cleansing light that will enable you to truly walk in freedom.

Eagle People...Today's reading is 1 John 2:1-5.
Pleya gi. "Go with Blessings."

<u>August 23</u>

Blinding Darkness

Know this warriors, the darkness is clearing away and true Light is being revealed. But be careful. Whoever claims to walk in the Light yet hates a fellow warrior is still walking in darkness. Whoever loves a fellow warrior is in the Light.

You can fully know whether you are walking in darkness or Light. Whoever loves their fellow warriors is in the Light and does not cause others to stumble on their path. But whoever hates or despises their fellow warriors is in the darkness and is walking around in the dark.

The warrior who hates does not understand or see where they are going because the darkness has blinded their eyes.

Eagle People...Today's reading is 1 John 2:6-11.
Pleya gi. "Go with Blessings."

August 24

Sensual Cravings

I am writing to you, young warriors, because for Creator Yahweh's name's sake your sins and wrong-doing have been forgiven and pardoned. I am writing to you mothers and fathers, because you have come to recognize and be aware of Creator Yahweh who has existed from the beginning. I am writing to all who have been victorious over the wicked one, that evil trickster, and because you are strong and the *Sacred Writings* abide in your hearts.

Do not love or cherish the world and the things of the world. Instead, continue to walk in the Spirit way, because the things of the world...the craving for sensual gratification and the lust of the eyes and greedy longings of the mind that always wants more and more, and the pride of relying on our own resources and strength...these things do not come from Creator Yahweh.

The entire world and all its desires will pass away! But the warrior who continues to walk the Spirit way will abide forever. Hold these promises deep in your hearts warriors, and let Holy Spirit power quicken you with strength and courage.

Eagle People...Today's reading is 1 John 2:12-17.
Pleya gi. "Go with Blessings."

August 25

The Last Hour

Know this warriors, this is the last hour. We are coming quickly to the end of the age. Many will fall away from our tribe and abandon the faith and follow those who claim to be in the Light but are not. Keep your hearts strong! These people who fall away did not truly belong to us, or they would have never left. They would have remained with us. But they have believed the lies of the evil trickster and have left the way of Light.

But you hold a sacred commission from Creator Yahweh, the Holy One, and you know the Truth. Continue to walk as eagle people, rising above the circumstances and trouble of this world. Take courage! Take strength! Holy Spirit power lives in you!

Eagle People...Today's reading is 1 John 2:18-24.
Pleya gi. "Go with Blessings."

August 26
A Sacred Appointment

Be careful warriors! There are many who would try to deceive you and lead you astray. But you have a sacred commission received from Creator Yahweh's Holy Spirit that abides in you forever. So, you have no need for anyone to instruct you. Spirit power teaches you concerning everything. This is how you know what is Truth and what is a lie from the evil trickster. Spirit power discerns for you.

Keep in your hearts what you have heard from the beginning... Creator Yahweh is Light and in him there is no darkness at all! He has promised restoration and eternal life and it will come, and not a day too late.

Eagle People...Today's reading is 1 John 2:25-27.
Pleya gi. "Go with Blessings."

August 27
Perfect Confidence

Remain in Holy Spirit power, warriors, and when Creator Yahweh is made visible you will not shrink back. You will enjoy perfect confidence and not shrink back or be ashamed at his coming, because you know that you have been bought with a price and that you belong to him.

If you perceive and know that Creator Yahweh is absolutely righteous then you know that whoever conforms to his will is born of him and is a child of God.

This is how we know that he lives in us...we know it by his Holy Spirit power that lives inside us.

Eagle People...Today's reading is 1 John 2:28-29.
Pleya gi. "Go with Blessings."

August 28

Perfect Love!

What incredible love Creator Yahweh has lavished on us! That we should be called children of God! And that is what we are! Beloved warriors, the reason the world does not recognize us is because it did not recognize Jesus Yeshua. They did not know him. But you know him and enjoy perfect peace in his presence.

Take time to bask in this peace, warriors, and rejoice in the uniqueness of how he made you. You are beautiful in his sight.

Praise Creator Yahweh for his perfect love that casts out all fear.

Eagle People...Today's reading is 1 John 3:1.
Pleya gi. "Go with Blessings."

August 29

Laying Down Our Lives

Warriors, this is the message you have heard from the beginning that we should love one another. You know that we have always been a giving people, sharing with any who are in need. Sharing possessions is a good way to show love.

This is how we know what love is. Jesus Yeshua laid down his life for us and we ought to lay down our lives for our brothers and sisters. If we see one of our cousins or relations in need and we have no pity, how can we say the love of Creator Yahweh is in us? Having no compassion only leads to death. We pass from death into life by loving our brothers and sisters.

Eagle People ... Today's reading is 1 John 3:2-17.
Pleya gi. "Go with Blessings."

August 30

Love in Action

Warriors, let us not love with words only, but in action and in truth. Do not make it your aim to love yourself. Make it your aim to love Creator Yahweh with all your heart, soul, mind, and strength. Then make it your second goal to love your fellow warriors, thinking of their needs above your own.

By truly loving others you will know that you belong to the truth, and your heart with be at rest in the presence of our Great Chief and Captain. Even when your heart condemns you (because you know what darkness lurks there), your heart can quickly be at rest, because Creator Yahweh is greater than our hearts, and he knows everything.

Eagle People...Today's reading is 1 John 3:18-20.
Pleya gi. "Go with Blessings."

August 31

Obedient Warriors

Warriors, since our hearts do not condemn us (because Creator Yahweh is greater than our hearts and he knows everything) then we have confidence and complete boldness before our great Chief and Captain and we know we will receive from him anything that we ask. This is because we obey his orders, follow his plan for us, and practice what is pleasing to him.

Creator Yahweh's commands are simple...to believe in the name of his Son, Jesus Yeshua, and to live and continue to live, and abide in him, and to love one another. Warriors who obey his commands live in him, and he in them.

How do we know he lives in us? We know it by the Spirit he gave us. Continue to walk in Holy Spirit power, warriors, and you will do well.

Eagle People...Today's reading is 1 John 3:21-24.
Pleya gi. "Go with Blessings."

Cobby Shadley
(Ghostdancer's brother)

September

September 1

Test The Spirit

We live by Spirit power and have long lived with one foot in both worlds. But warriors, do not believe every spirit. Test the spirits to see whether they are from Creator Yahweh or not.

This is how you can recognize the Spirit of Creator Yahweh: Every spirit that acknowledges that Jesus Yeshua has come in the flesh is from Creator Yahweh, but every spirit that does not acknowledge Jesus Yeshua is not from Creator Yahweh. This is the spirit of the antichrist, the ultimate trickster, which you have heard is coming and even now is already in the world.

Keep alert! Continue to read the *Sacred Writings*. This will help you as you test the spirits to know which Spirit is from Creator Yahweh and which spirits are from the evil one.

Eagle People...Today's reading is 1 John 4:1-3.
Pleya gi. "Go with Blessings."

September 2

Listen to Spirit

Warriors, you belong to Creator Yahweh! Because of this you have already overcome the spirits sent out by the evil trickster. Don't let anyone take you back into slavery and don't be led astray by the evil one.

The Holy Spirit who lives in you is greater and mightier than the one who is in the world. Whoever is of the world listens to the spirit of the world, which is the evil trickster, but whoever belongs to Creator Yahweh listens to those who speak his Words.

This is how you can recognize the Spirit of truth and the spirit of falsehood. Stay strong in the *Sacred Writings* and you will easily discern the difference.

Eagle People...Today's reading is 1 John 4:4-6.
Pleya gi. "Go with Blessings."

September 3
Wellsprings of Love

Warriors! Let us love one another! Love is a wellspring that comes from Creator Yahweh. Everyone who loves has been born of Creator Yahweh and recognizes and knows him as our Great Chief and Captain. Whoever does not love does not recognize Creator Yahweh, because Creator Yahweh is love.

This is how our Great Chief and Captain showed his love among us: He sent his one and only Son, Jesus Yeshua, into the world that we might live through him.

This is love: not that we loved our Great Chief and Captain, but that he loved us and sent his Son as an atoning sacrifice for every wrong thing we have ever done.

Eagle People...Today's reading is 1 John 4:7-11.
Pleya gi. "Go with Blessings."

September 4
Rely on Love

Warriors, we are Spirit people! It is an amazing thing that we live and move and have our being in Creator Yahweh, but that he also lives in us! Creator Yahweh has sent his Son, Jesus Yeshua, to be the Savior of the world.

We know and rely on the love our Great Chief and Captain has for us.

Since Creator Yahweh so loved us, we also ought to love one another. No one has ever seen Creator Yahweh; but if we love each other, his love is made complete in us because he lives in us.

Creator Yahweh is love. Whoever lives in love lives in Creator Yahweh and Creator Yahweh lives in him. What an amazing thing! Let us dance our prayers before him, knowing full well that he hears every cry of our heart. Yahweh. Yahweh. Yahweh. Praise our Great Chief and Captain.

Eagle People...Today's reading is 1 John 4:12-16.
Pleya gi. "Go with Blessings."

September 5

When Our Hearts Condemn Us

I have had much to say about love, warriors, but there is still more. Creator Yahweh's love is made complete in us so that we will have confidence on the day of judgment. In this world we are like him.

Even when our hearts condemn us, we can know and have confidence because of his Spirit that lives in us. There is no fear in love. Creator Yahweh's perfect love drives out all fear. How can we fear punishment when Jesus Yeshua has taken all of our punishment for us?

The warrior who fears is not made perfect in love. If you still fear judgment, climb the Sacred Mountain (whether in body or spirit) and fall before your great Chief and Captain. He will welcome you with open arms. Lay down your quiver and bow and bask in the perfect love that drives out all fear.

Eagle People...Today's reading is 1 John 4:17-18.
Pleya gi. "Go with Blessings."

September 6

Two Commands

Warriors, we love one another because Creator Yahweh first loved us. He has made it possible for our hearts to hold and share love. If any warrior says, "I love Creator Yahweh," yet hates his brother, the truth is not in him. For any warrior who cannot love his own brother, whom he has seen, cannot possibly love Creator Yahweh, whom he has not seen.

Remember, Creator Yahweh has given us two commands: to love Him and to love our fellow warriors. Whoever loves Creator Yahweh must also love his brothers.

Eagle People...Today's reading is 1 John 4:19-21.
Pleya gi. "Go with Blessings."

September 7

Overcome The World

Warriors, I have a little more to say on the matter of loving our fellow warriors. Everyone who believes that Jesus Yeshua is the Christ is born of Creator Yahweh, and every warrior who loves the father loves the father's child. This is how we know that we love Creator Yahweh's children: by loving Creator Yahweh and loving each other. If we love each other, then we have overcome the world.

Our faith is what makes us victorious over the world! Warriors who believe that Jesus Yeshua is the Son of Creator Yahweh have overcome the world. It is the Holy Spirit that testifies of this to us, because the Spirit that lives in us is Truth.

Eagle People...Today's reading is 1 John 5:1-6.
Pleya gi. "Go with Blessings."

September 8

The Testimony

Warriors, anyone who believes in Jesus Yeshua, that he is the Son of our Great Chief and Captain believes the testimony that He gives regarding his own Son.

Whoever does not believe this has made Creator Yahweh out to be a liar, because he has not believed the testimony of our great Chief and Captain.

And this is the testimony: Our Great Chief and Captain has given us eternal life, and this life is in his Son, Jesus Yeshua. Warriors who have the Son have life. Warriors who do not have the Son of our Great Chief and Captain do not have life.

Remember, do not let your heart condemn you. If you acknowledge that Jesus Yeshua is the Son of our Great Chief and Captain, then you have the gift of eternal life. You know this because you are a spiritual people and Creator Yahweh's Spirit lives in you.

Eagle People...Today's reading is 1 John 5:7-12.
Pleya gi. "Go with Blessings."

September 9

Amazing News!

Warriors, thank you for putting up with this talk about love. I write these things to you because you believe in the name of Jesus Yeshua, the Son of our Great Chief and Captain and I want you to know that you have eternal life.

Because of this we can have assurance when approaching our Great Chief and Captain that he hears us. He hears every cry of our hearts. And we can have whatever we ask of him because we are asking according to his will for us.

This is a most wonderful thing. Creator Yahweh has cleansed our hearts and has made it so that our hearts will not condemn us. He has called us his children! And he has made it possible for us to enter before his throne fearless and loved. This is amazing news! Let us lift up our prayers of thankfulness to our Great Chief and Captain.

Eagle People...Today's reading is 1 John 5:13-15.
Pleya gi. "Go with Blessings."

September 10

Protected!

Warriors, we need to pray for one another. If you see your fellow warrior walking in error or doing something wrong, pray for him! All wrongdoing is sin, and we know that warriors born of Creator Yahweh do not continue to walk the sin way.

Yes. We make mistakes. Yes. Our hearts sometimes condemn us. But we come back to the Father, our Great Chief and Captain and his son, Creator Yahweh, and his love casts out all fear.

Anyone who continues to walk the sin way, day after day, mile after mile, is not born of Creator Yahweh, because we know that anyone who is born of Creator Yahweh does not continue to sin. The evil one cannot touch such a warrior because they are protected by Spirit power.

Eagle People...Today's reading is 1 John 5:16-18.
Pleya gi. "Go with Blessings."

September 11

In Him Who is True!

Warriors, now we know that we are the children of Creator Yahweh. Hold this assurance in your heart. The whole world is under the control of the wicked one, that evil trickster, but we are not under his control. Jesus Yeshua has given us understanding, so that we may know and understand and continue to know better and more clearly him who is true. And not only that, we are IN him who is true. He is the true Creator and Life Eternal.

Dear warriors, keep yourselves from anything and everything that would fill the place in your heart that belongs only to Creator Yahweh. Let no substitute take first place in your life. This is the way of walking in beauty.

Eagle People...Today's reading is 1 John 5:19-21.
Pleya gi. "Go with Blessings."

September 12

Wholly Devoted

In view of Creator Yahweh's great mercies that are renewed every morning, or simply because of all that he has done for you, warriors, present your body, mind, spirit and soul to him. Honor him as your Great Chief and Captain! Give him control of your life every morning as the sun rises over the hill. Continue giving control to him as the sun walks its path across the heavens, being wholly devoted and consecrated to please him.

Pleasing our Great Chief and Captain is not difficult warriors. Though his ways are much higher than ours, and his thoughts beyond our understanding, his commands are simple and he gives us Spirit power to follow them. He does not weigh us down with many rules, but simply asks that we obey him by loving him first and then loving others.

Eagle People...Today's reading is
Romans 12:1 & Isaiah 33:2.
Pleya gi. "Go with Blessings."

<u>September 13</u>

Transformed Thinking

Creator Yahweh is the Merciful One. Do not conform to the ways of the world and how the world thinks. Transform your thinking by renewing your mind, which comes from diving deep into the *Sacred Writings*. Let his Word wash you and fill you until you are completely submerged with Truth.

When your soul is bowed down and continually in remembrance of your misery as an outcast, dive into the *Sacred Writings* and rediscover the hope and expectation that Creator Yahweh has given us. It is because of his great mercy and loving kindness that we are not consumed. His compassion and mercy never fail.

Trust in him, warrior, and live every day as an act of worship.

Eagle People...Today's reading is
Lamentations 3:19-23 & Romans 12:2.
Pleya gi. "Go with Blessings."

<u>September 14</u>

My Portion

Warriors, are you having trouble trusting Creator Yahweh? I am a man who has seen affliction by the rod of my Great Chief and Captain's wrath.

In the past he has driven me away and made me walk in darkness rather than light; indeed, he has turned his hand against me again and again, all day long, but he always does this out of his great mercy. And I remember that he is good to those who wait hopefully and expectantly for him. It is good to inquire of him according to the authority of his *Sacred Writings*.

Yes we can trust him. Because of his great mercies we are not consumed, though we often deserve it. His compassions never fail. They are new with the rising of each sun. Great is the faithfulness of our Great Chief and Captain. I say to myself, "The Lord is my portion, therefore I will wait for him."

Eagle People...Today's reading is Lamentations 3:1-24.
Pleya gi. "Go with Blessings."

September 15

He Will Come Near

Warriors, there is a time to fight! And there is a time to wait quietly for the salvation of our Great Chief and Captain. For no one is cast off by Creator Yahweh forever. Though he brings grief, he will show compassion, so great is his unfailing love. For he does not willingly bring affliction or grief to anyone.

Let us examine our ways and test them, and let us return to Creator Yahweh. Let us lift up our hearts and our hands to Creator in heaven, and say, "We have sinned and rebelled." Because of the blood of Jesus Yeshua he will forgive us. He will come near when we call upon him.

Eagle People...Today's reading is Lamentations 3:25-59.
Pleya gi. "Go with Blessings."

September 16

Justice Streams Down

Know this warriors, People who do evil do not fear our Great Chief and Captain. They think of themselves so highly that they don't even know that what they are doing is wrong. Lies come out of their mouths and wisdom is far from them.

Everything they do and think is tainted by darkness.In spite of this, Creator Yahweh's love reaches to the heavens, his faithfulness to the skies. His righteousness rises above us like a mighty sacred mountain, and his justice streams down in waves of falling water. He preserves both man and beast. Both high and low find refuge in the shadow of Creator Yahweh's wings.

Eagle People...Today's reading is Psalm 36:1-7.
Pleya gi. "Go with Blessings."

September 17

Beauty of Dance

Warriors, do you realize how valuable and precious is the love of our Great Chief and Captain? His love is dependable and steadfast and never wavering. The children of men take refuge beneath the shadow of his wings knowing he will provide every good thing for them. For even in sorrow and affliction, his love remains true. And even in the deepest pit he fills us with great hope for tomorrow.

Creator Yahweh is the fountain of life and it is in his Light that we truly see light. This Light is where hope is birthed. His loving-kindness covers all who know him, and his righteousness flows over the upright in heart. Don't worry about those who do evil. They will one day fall and lie prostrate. They will be thrust down by the hand of Creator Yahweh and will never rise again. But you, warriors, will rise to sing the glory of our Great Chief and Captain. How can we do less than praise him now in the beauty of our dance?

Eagle People...Today's reading is Psalm 36:7-12.
Pleya gi. "Go with Blessings."

September 18

Hold Onto Hope

Warriors, do not fret over evil people who love walking in the darkness. Don't be envious when you see these evil people prospering. For like the grass, they will soon wilt, like green plants they will soon die away.

Hold onto your hope and continue walking the Beauty Way. Trust in Creator Yahweh with all your heart and continue to do good and you will dwell in the land and enjoy safe pasture. Delight yourself in your Great Chief and Captain and he will give you the desires of your heart. What joy you will find, walking in the Blessing Way, when you realize the very things you love to do are exactly what Creator Yahweh wants you to do.

Eagle People...Today's reading is Psalm 37:1-4.
Pleya gi. "Go with Blessings."

September 19

Lean Your Whole Weight

Warriors, as you continue walking the Beauty Way each day, as the sun rises over the hill, commit your way to Creator Yahweh. He will make your right standing with him shine like the noonday sun! Others will see and know that you belong to your Great Chief and Captain.

It is a good thing to find a place of rest for your weary soul and to be still and rest in Creator Yahweh. Lean your whole weight into him.

In this way you will be able to cease from anger and forsake wrath. Do not allow yourself to fall into a pit of worry, because anger, bitterness and worry will only lead you to the dark side where those who do evil dwell. Those evildoers shall be cut off, but those who wait and hope and look for Creator Yahweh will one day inherit the earth.

Eagle People...Today's reading is Psalm 37:5-9.
Pleya gi. "Go with Blessings."

September 20

Swords of The Wicked

A little while and evildoers will be no more; though you search through the forest high and low, they will not be found. But the humble of heart will inherit the land and delight themselves in the abundance of peace.

Do not worry about evildoers who plot against you and gnash their teeth at you; for Creator Yahweh laughs at the wicked and he knows their day is coming. They may take aim at you to bring you down and even kill you, but Creator Yahweh laughs at them and orders the number of their days just as he does with you.

The swords of the wicked shall enter their own hearts and their bows shall be broken. Your day is also coming soon, warriors, a day of unceasing delights in the presence of our Great Chief and Captain. Let us shout aloud for joy! And dance our prayers to Creator Yahweh.

Eagle People...Today's reading is Psalm 37:10-15.
Pleya gi. "Go with Blessings."

September 21

Satisfied

It is better to have little and stand without compromise in our faith in Creator Yahweh than it is to have a great many possessions and do wrong. Our Great Chief and Captain will break the arms of the wicked while he upholds those who consistently look to him for their strength. Those warriors who walk this way in Beauty shall not be put to shame in the time of evil; and in the days of famine they shall be satisfied.

Such people who are blessed of Creator Yahweh shall inherit the earth, but they that are cursed of him will be cut off. The only ones who are cursed of him are those who have made a decision to walk outside his path of beauty.

All of us used to walk in this way of darkness, but then we gave our lives over to our Great Chief and Captain. The steps of a good warrior are directed and established by Creator Yahweh because such a warrior delights in our Great Chief and Captain!

Eagle People...Today's reading is Psalm 37:16-19.
Pleya gi. "Go with Blessings."

September 22

Give Generously

Warriors we are to give generously of all that Creator Yahweh has given us. The gifts of healing and life breath are ours to give. The gifts of provision and shelter are ours to share. The gifts of wisdom and direction are available to all who dive into the *Sacred Writings*. We have always been a giving people, let us be more so as our Great Chief and Captain pours out his love into our hearts.

This way of walking in Beauty will keep your steps firm as you delight in your Creator. Though you may stumble, you will not fall, for Creator Yahweh upholds you with his mighty hand.

Eagle People...Today's reading is Psalm 37:20-24.
Pleya gi. "Go with Blessings."

September 23

Sold-Out Warriors

Warriors, I have been young and I have been old, yet I have never seen any warrior who is completely sold out to Creator Yahweh forsaken. Neither are their offspring forsaken or begging for food.

From the rising of the sun in the east and as it marks its path across the heavens, even when it falls below the far mountain and sinks into darkness these sold-out warriors are merciful and deal graciously with everyone. They lend all good things and their offspring are blessed.

Trust in Creator Yahweh! Lean on him. Rely on him. Find your confidence in him. This is the way you and your offspring will dwell in the land and feed on his faithfulness. Delight yourself in him and he will grant the secret petitions of your heart.

Eagle People...Today's reading is Psalm 37:25-26.
Pleya gi. "Go with Blessings."

September 24

A Secure Stronghold

Remember warriors, Creator Yahweh will not forsake his faithful ones! Yes, we see wicked men in great power and spreading themselves like a green tree in its native soil, but they have no promise of a future hope. You will look for them but not find them for they will be cut off, never to be found. These wicked ones will be destroyed together.

Salvation belongs to Creator's warriors who are made righteous through the blood of Jesus Yeshua. Wicked people may be able to crush the body, but they cannot destroy the soul. Creator Yahweh is our Refuge and secure Stronghold in times of trouble. He will help us and deliver us because we trust and take refuge in him. We will not be left in the hands of the wicked, for our Great Chief and Captain carries us on his wings.

Eagle People...Today's reading is Psalm 37:27-40.
Pleya gi. "Go with Blessings."

September 25

Gracious & Kind

I love Creator Yahweh because he always hears my voice. He has heard my cry for mercy and has turned his ear to me. I will call on him as long as I live.

The cords of death entangled me. I was overcome by dread of the place of the dead. I walked the way of sorrow. But then, I called on the name of my Great Chief and Captain, "Save me!" He parted the heavens and came down. He drew me out of many waters.

Creator Yahweh is gracious and kind. He is completely righteous and forgiving. When I was brought low, he saved me. Return to your rest, weary warriors, for Creator Yahweh has been good to you.

Eagle People...Today's reading is Psalm 116:1-7.
Pleya gi. "Go with Blessings."

September 26
Deliverance

Creator Yahweh has delivered me from death. He has dried the tears from my eyes and kept my feet from falling off the good path that I may continue to walk the way of Beauty.

I have told him all my problems and trusted them into his care. I believed, trusted in, relied on, and am still clinging to Creator Yahweh. He is my Great Chief and Captain. Therefore, my tongue will praise his name all the days of my life. You can trust him warriors, he cares for you.

Eagle People...Today's reading is Psalm 116:8-10.
Pleya gi. "Go with Blessings."

September 27
Undeserving Favor

Warriors, how can we possibly repay Creator Yahweh for all the good things he has done for us? Each day the sun greets us with its warmth. At night we lie down beneath the sheltering shadows. Each breath we take reminds us that we are alive! What vows have you made to our Great Chief and Captain?

It is a good thing to fulfill those vows in the sight of all our people. Let them know of his goodness and mercy. Let them know that he hears their cries for mercy. Let them know that precious in his sight is the death of his warriors. He has freed us from our chains!

Call on his name and offer your prayers of thanks. Dance before him as one who has found undeserving favor.

Eagle People...Today's reading is Psalm 116:11-19.
Pleya gi. "Go with Blessings."

September 28
Confident Expectation

Warriors, I pray grace over you, and spiritual blessing, and peace falling like rain over you from Creator Yahweh. He is the Father of compassion and the Source of every comfort and consolation and encouragement. Our Great Chief and Captain comforts us in our sorrows so that we can comfort others who walk the sorrow way. Yes. The sufferings of Jesus Yeshua flow over us, but his comfort also overflows over us like a river reaching all who come in contact with us.

This knowledge gives me hope for you and confident expectation and unwavering assurance that you will be comforted, and not a moment too late. Yes, we have felt the sentence of death, but these things happen to us so that we will not rely on our own strength or intellect or courage, but that we will rely on Creator Yahweh who raises the dead. He will rescue us! Place your hope and confident expectation on him.

Eagle People...Today's reading is 2 Corinthians 1:2-9.
Pleya gi. "Go with Blessings."

September 29

Nurture The Spirit

Yes, warriors, Creator Yahweh raises the dead, and we were once dead in the way we used to live. But we were created to be a spiritual people. Therefore, the nurture of the Spirit ought to be a priority in our lives. Every day we should dive into the *Sacred Writings* and let them take root in our soul. By living in such a way we leave fleshly wisdom behind and walk in the grace of Creator Yahweh with sincerity and a pure heart.

This is a choice and not a difficult thing to do, for it is our Great Chief and Captain that keeps, strengthens and delivers us from the old way of walking in darkness.

Call on Creator Yahweh for help! For his promises are always "yes," and he has anointed us and set his seal upon us. Not only that, but he has also placed his Holy Spirit in our hearts as a deposit of what is to come. It is our Great Chief and Captain who gives us the strength and ability to continue walking in the way of Beauty. Praise him with your whole heart. He reigns above all!

Eagle People...Today's reading is 2 Corinthians 1:10-22.
Pleya gi. "Go with Blessings."

<u>September 30</u>

The Light Has Dawned

Warriors, long ago our people walked in darkness as did all the people of the earth, but now we have seen a great Light. This great Light of Jesus Yeshua has even dawned upon the dead. That is why we are now alive! Creator Yahweh has enlarged our nation and increased our joy! Our people are rising up again to serve our Great Chief and Captain in the unique way he has made us.

Creator Yahweh is our Wonderful Counselor. We can go to him with any question, any need. He is our Mighty God. We can trust him to forever be faithful and true. He is our Everlasting Father. He will not leave us as orphans, but holds an eternal inheritance for us. And He is our Prince of Peace. Let peace reign in our hearts as we celebrate the joy of our Great Chief and Captain.

Eagle People...Today's reading is Isaiah 9:1-6.
Pleya gi. "Go with Blessings."

166

Elissa Peacock

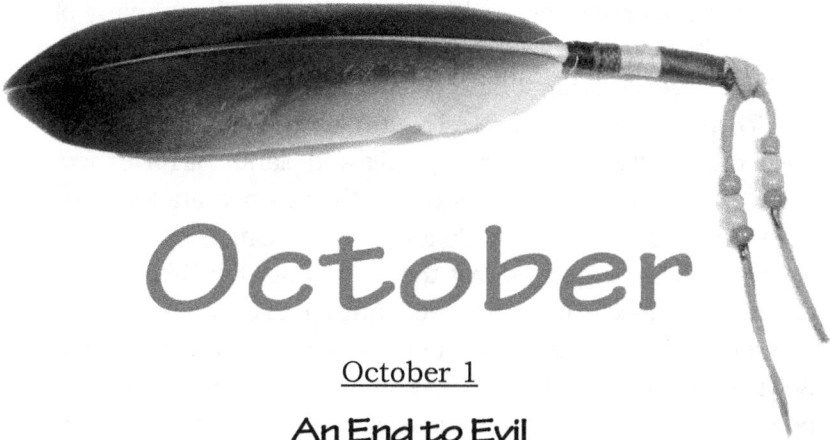

October

October 1

An End to Evil

Warriors consider this...there is an end to evil. It had a beginning and it will have an end. As Spirit people we look forward to the day when the peace of Creator Yahweh will reign forever! He had no beginning and he has no end and his peace will reign eternal. He will put all his enemies under his feet and will abolish death forevermore.

This is the hope to which we have been called. Yet, now, as we walk along the surface of the earth, we face death every day. We see the death of our dreams, of our strength, and our bodies. But we need never lose hope!

Our Great Chief and Captain has promised life to us and eternal joy! This is enough to keep us walking the Beauty Way.

Eagle People...Today's reading is
Isaiah 9:7 & 1 Corinthians 15:25-30.
Pleya gi. "Go with Blessings."

October 2

Alive For The First Time

Warriors, we die daily. The world tells us we must find ourselves and that we must love ourselves before we can love others. But Creator Yahweh has told us that we must first love others. He has also said that unless a seed falls to the ground and dies it cannot bring forth new life.

169

Like that seed, we die to the old way of walking in darkness. We die to evil desires and selfish gain. We even die to many of our dreams, but like that seed that falls to the ground, we spring up in new life. Alive for the first time!

There are heavenly bodies of sun, moon, and stars, and there are earthly bodies of humans, animals and plants. All have their own glory. The sun is glorious in one way, the moon in another, and the stars even more distinctive. So it is with us. Our body that is sown is perishable and decays, but the body that Our Great Chief and Captain will raise is imperishable, immune to decay, and immortal! Sown in dishonor and humiliation; it is raised in honor and glory. Sown in weakness, raised in strength and power. Sown a natural body, raised a spiritual body. This is a blessed hope that keeps us walking the Beauty Way.

Eagle People...Today's reading is 1 Corinthians 15:31-44. *Pleya gi.* "Go with Blessings."

<u>October 3</u>

Walking Between Two Worlds

Warriors, the *Sacred Writings* teach us that the first man was formed out of the earth. He was made of dust and represents all who follow after and are earthly minded. The Second Man is from heaven, Jesus Yeshua. We who follow him as our Great Chief and Captain are also of heaven and so become heavenly minded. We no longer think only of earthly things; we walk between two worlds.

In the past we bore the image of the man of dust, but now we bear the image of the Man of heaven. The first man Adam became a living being. The last Adam, Jesus Yeshua, became a life-giving Spirit, restoring the dead to life. Do you feel it warriors? We have already been restored! We are already seated with Creator Yahweh in heavenly places. Take courage. This is a spiritual mystery, but we will one day see it with our own eyes.

Eagle People...Today's reading is 1 Corinthians 15:45-50. *Pleya gi.* "Go with Blessings."

<u>October 4</u>

Your Light Has Come!

Arise and shine warriors! Your Light has come! And the glory of Creator Yahweh shines upon you. You have been depressed and walking through thick darkness that has covered our people, but the Light of our Great Chief and Captain is rising upon us. His glory falls like a blanket about all who call upon him, covering all our wrong-doings and making us shine like stars.

Nations will come to your Light, and kings to the brightness of your rising dawn. What a glorious day when you lift up your eyes and see all that is round about you. All the gathering nations will see you shining bright. Your heart shall leap for joy when you see your sons and daughters coming from afar. This is the hope of all who are covered with the precious blood of Jesus Yeshua.

Eagle People...Today's reading is Isaiah 60:1-7.
Pleya gi. "Go with Blessings."

<u>October 5</u>

A Great Mystery!

I tell you a great mystery, warriors, we shall not all fall asleep in death. We shall be transformed! In a moment, in the twinkling of an eye. The part of us that can die will put on that which cannot die, and the mortal part of us shall put on immortality. And when we experience this freedom from death, we will realize the fulfillment of the promise that death is swallowed up forever in victory.

On that day Creator Yahweh will destroy the covering of mourning that has been cast over our people. He will swallow up death and wipe away tears from our faces. On that day we will say, "Behold our Great Chief and Captain upon Whom we have waited and hoped, that He might save us! This is Creator Yahweh. We have waited for Him and we will be glad and rejoice in his salvation."

This is a great promise, warriors, for all who put their trust and hope in Creator Yahweh. Stand strong! Do not waiver from walking in Beauty.

Eagle People...Today's reading is
1 Corinthians 15:51-55 & Isaiah 25:7-9.
Pleya gi. "Go with Blessings."

October 6

Walk in The Way

Stand firm warriors! Let nothing move you. Serve your Great Chief and Captain with your whole heart and ability. Whatever you are sure he has placed on your heart, do it. When he speaks to you in dreams and visions of the night, answer him. When you hear his voice saying, "This is the way, walk in it," obey him. He is worthy of our trust.

Creator Yahweh has created you unique and gifted you with unique gifts. Make it your aim to discover those gifts and use them for his glory! And whatever you do, do it in love, never forgetting to love your Great Chief and Captain and to love others. These are his two great commands.

Eagle People...Today's reading is 1 Corinthians 15:56-58. *Pleya gi.* "Go with Blessings."

October 7

Bold Warriors

Warriors, we are called to warfare, but do not mistake your enemy! We do not fight against flesh and blood. Be careful to not strike out against your brothers and sisters. Our fight is against the powers and master spirits who rule this present darkness. We war against the spirit forces of wickedness in the spirit realm. This kind of war requires the full armor of Creator Yahweh, so that on the dangerous day of evil we will be able to stand.

Stand, therefore, as bold warriors, and do not allow your minds to become quickly unsettled or disturbed or alarmed. Let no one deceive or mislead you in any way. For there will come a great falling away of those who have professed to follow Creator Yahweh. Stand firm and do not let yourselves be led astray. Keep your spiritual fire, serving our Great Chief and Captain and encourage one another as you see the day approaching.

Eagle People ... Today's reading is 2 Thessalonians 2:1-3.
Pleya gi. "Go with Blessings."

October 8

Here For A Purpose

Be alert warriors and stand your guard. Act like the strong warriors you are and be courageous! Let everything be done in the true love of Creator Yahweh, love him first and love others through his love for you. Stand firm and hold fast to the traditions and instructions, which you have been taught through Holy Spirit power and *Sacred Writings.*

Be content with what you have, for Creator Yahweh has long ago ordained the land we shall possess right to its very borders. Do not hide your face. He is using you right where you are. You are here for a purpose, so make it your aim to be loyal to our Great Chief and Captain. Whether you are out on the front lines of battle or alone as a lookout, stand firm and true. Creator Yahweh is trustworthy and faithful.

Eagle People...Today's reading is 2 Thessalonians 2:13-15.
Pleya gi. "Go with Blessings."

October 9

Beyond Our Circumstances

Sometimes, warriors, Creator Yahweh seems very far away. We cry out in the daytime, yet he answers not and seems to have forsaken us. We groan throughout the night yet he remains silent. It is times like these we must remember that he is holy and faithful and just. We must look beyond our circumstances and see him high and lifted up in the Holy Place beyond the Sacred Mountain.

We must also look to our ancestors and remember that they trusted in our Great Chief and Captain. They were confident even in the silent times while walking the Sorrow Way. Creator Yahweh delivered them. They cried out and were delivered and were not ashamed or disappointed. Sometimes their hope was realized in this life, but often it came when they crossed over, freed from the chains that held them. And they received honor because of their steadfastness.

Keep calling out, fellow warriors, and let his Spirit comfort you at just the right time.

Eagle People...Today's reading is Psalm 22:1-5.
Pleya gi. "Go with Blessings."

October 10

In The Day of Trouble

Warriors, I pray that Creator Yahweh will answer you in the day of trouble! May our Great Chief and Captain set you in a spacious place and defend you from all your enemies. May he send you help from the Sacred Mountain and support you in your work as you serve him. May he refresh and strengthen you in Spirit power. May he grant you your true heart's desire.

The day will come, warriors, when we will shout in triumph at the victory of our Great Chief and Captain, and in that day we will lift up banners in the name of Creator Yahweh.

Some boast in chariots and some trust in their horses, but we trust in the name of Creator Yahweh. Let our voices shout in praise and our feet dance in a song of celebration. Yahweh. Yahweh. Yahweh. He is always faithful and true.

Eagle People...Today's reading is Psalm 20.
Pleya gi. "Go with Blessings."

October 11

Clearly Seen

The Heavens declare the glory of Creator Yahweh; the skies proclaim the work of his hands. Day after day they pour forth speech. There is no tongue or language where their voice is not heard. Their voice goes into all the earth. Have you not heard this voice, warriors? The shout is loud and strong!

The heavens also reveal the wrath of our Great Chief and Captain poured out against all the godlessness and wickedness of people who repress and hinder the truth. For that which is known about Creator Yahweh is evident and made plain in their inner consciousness, because Creator Yahweh has made it plain to them.

For since the creation of the world Creator Yahweh's invisible qualities—his eternal power and holy nature—have been clearly seen by everyone. Open your eyes, warriors, and see the One who called you by name. Let the mighty wind of his Holy Spirit restore you from deep within.

Eagle People...Today's reading is
Psalm 19: 1-3 & Romans 1:18-20.
Pleya gi. "Go with Blessings."

October 12

A Time for Healing

Warriors, it is time to break up the barren ground! Let us sow for ourselves righteousness that comes through the blood of Jesus Yeshua. Then we will reap the fruit of unfailing love. It is time to seek Creator Yahweh. He has showered us with his righteousness and rained his salvation upon us.

In the past we have eaten the fruit of deception and lies. Because we trusted in our own strength and in the strength of our many warriors, the roar of battle rose against our people.

The time for healing has come. Creator Yahweh has led us with chords of human kindness and with ties of love. He rises to show compassion on us and desires to lift the yoke of bondage from our necks. There is healing in his mighty wings. Let us respond by sowing compassion.

Eagle People...Today's reading is Hosea 10:12-11:4.
Pleya gi. "Go with Blessings."

October 13

The Holy One!

Warriors our Great Chief and Captain is God and not a man. He is a Spiritual Being, even The Great Spirit whom we have long known. He is Creator Yahweh, the Holy One among us. He roars like a mighty lion and when he roars, his children will come trembling and eagerly from the west. They will come trembling like birds from the east, like doves from the north. With loving kindness he will settle us in our homes.

Therefore, let us return to Creator Yahweh, the Lord our God. Let us hold fast to love and mercy. Let us cling to righteousness and justice, and let us wait expectantly for our Great Chief and Captain. It is he who heals us and not another.

Let us continue walking the Beauty Way with a heart of thankfulness and yearning. He is close warriors, let us reach out to him.

Eagle People...Today's reading is Hosea 11:5-12:6.
Pleya gi. "Go with Blessings."

October 14

Walk in Wisdom

Creator Yahweh is the Lord our God. He brought us out of the barren land and cared for us in the desert. He took care of us there in the land of burning heat. He fed us and we were satisfied, but then we became proud and forgot the One who made us.

Warriors, it is time to take words and return to Our Great Chief and Captain. Let us seek his council and ask him to forgive all our wrong doings. Let us beg him to pour out his grace upon us and receive us once again. Let us determine to not mount warhorses.

Let us never again say "our gods" to what our own hands have made. For it is in Creator Yahweh that the fatherless find compassion.

Creator Yahweh will heal all our waywardness and shower us with love. If we are wise, we will realize these things. If we are discerning, we will understand them.

The ways of Creator Yahweh are right. Those who are covered with his righteousness walk in his ways, but the rebellious stumble in them.

Eagle People...Today's reading is Hosea 13:1-14:9.
Pleya gi. "Go with Blessings."

October 15

A Profound Mark

Creator Yahweh reigns. Let the earth be glad. Let all his people rejoice! Clouds and thick darkness surround him just as they did at Mount Sinai when he met with Moses. Righteousness and justice are the foundation of his throne. Fire goes before him and consumes his enemies on every side. His lightning lights up the world; the earth sees and trembles. The mountains melt like wax before Creator Yahweh, before the Lord of all the earth.

Warriors, we can trust someone like this. He is able, through Spirit power, to energize and equip us with enough strength individually and as a nation to make a profound mark upon history!

Stand strong! He can take our biggest disappointments and turn them into rich jewels. He will come, and not a moment too late.

Eagle People...Today's reading is Psalm 97:1-5.
Pleya gi. "Go with Blessings."

October 16

Faithful Ones

Let those who love Creator Yahweh hate evil, for he guards the lives of his faithful ones. He delivers his faithful ones from the hand of the wicked. His Light shines upon those he has made righteous through Jesus Yeshua's blood. He pours out his joy on the upright in heart. Rejoice in your Great Chief and Captain and praise his holy name!

Day after day the heavens proclaim the righteousness of our Great Chief and Captain. All the peoples see his glory. For Creator Yahweh is the Great Spirit over all the earth. He is exalted above all gods. Worship him, warriors, and give him the honor due his mighty name.

Eagle People...Today's reading is Psalm 97:6-12.
Pleya gi. "Go with Blessings."

October 17

Let Love Abound

Warriors, when we gave our lives to Creator Yahweh he began a good work in us. He will keep up this good work until the return of Jesus Yeshua. You can trust him. He will be faithful to complete it. You need only to look to him for your strength instead of relying on your own.

So, let our love abound more and more and extend to its fullest measure in knowledge and depth of insight. Let us encourage one another in walking the Beauty Way.

Then we will be able to discern what is right and vital and excellent and pursue such things with all our strength and courage. In this way we will keep ourselves from stumbling and will not cause anyone else to stumble.

Let us become standing trees, producing fruit to feed the ones we love. In this way even our enemies will eat and be filled and some will be won over. Remember, warriors, we were once enemies to the cause of Creator Yahweh. Wherever there is a breath of life, there is still hope.

Eagle People...Today's reading is Philippians 1:1-11.
Pleya gi. "Go with Blessings."

October 18

Speak The Word!

Warriors, in these last days we will have trouble, but do not fear. You have given your hearts, your very lives, to Creator Yahweh and he is faithful and true. He will give us the courage to make it through the coming storm.

Even if we end up in chains, we must speak the Word of our Great Chief and Captain more courageously and fearlessly than ever!

We should never do this out of selfish ambition or while pointing a finger. It is important that we do this because love rules in our hearts. The love of Creator Yahweh constrains us to warn of the coming danger and give hope to the hopeless. And we must all remember where we came from. Let us remember that once our hearts, too, were far from walking in Beauty.

Let us love one another, and all the more as the Day approaches. Through Spirit power we will have sufficient courage to walk the Blessing Way.

Eagle People...Today's reading is Philippians 1:12-20.
Pleya gi. "Go with Blessings."

October 19

Finish The Work

Warriors, whatever happens in your life, whether good or bad, conduct yourself in a manner worthy of our Great Chief and Captain. If we live, we live for Jesus Yeshua. If we die, let us die for what is right! It is important to finish the work Creator Yahweh has given us to do. He will direct the hours of our lives if we allow.

We should stand together as one people, united in love and standing firm in One Spirit. We should not be frightened in any way by those who oppose us. Yes, we will suffer, that has been granted to us along with the exceeding great promises, but we can also rejoice! For to live is Christ and to die is gain. Our Great Chief and Captain has not left us defenseless, but has filled us with Spirit Power to overcome our enemies in the Day of Evil.

Let us encourage one another with these words from the *Sacred Writings,* especially as we see the Day fast approaching.

Eagle People...Today's reading is Philippians 1:21-30.
Pleya gi. "Go with Blessings."

October 20

Live in Harmony

Be careful, warriors. Do nothing out of selfish ambition or that is prompted by conceit and empty arrogance. You have heard it said, that you should love yourselves before you can love others, but that is not the Beauty Way.

When we love Creator Yahweh with all our heart and soul and mind and strength, and when we love others, then we will have a healthy love for ourselves that has nothing to do with selfishness or arrogance.

Let us strengthen, console, and encourage one another, stirring up each other's gifts. Let us live in soul harmony by being of the same mind and one in purpose in serving our Great Chief and Captain. Let us consider others better than ourselves and look to their interests as well as our own.

We are a family, all related to Creator Yahweh, let us honor and respect one another. In doing so we will be united in the love of Christ, receiving comfort and fellowship with the Holy Spirit and walking in joy!

Eagle People...Today's reading is Philippians 2:1-4.
Pleya gi. "Go with Blessings."

October 21

Proclaim His Love!

W arriors, do not forget that we should have the same attitude as that of Creator Yahweh. He is equal with our Great Chief and Captain yet he humbled himself and became one of us, even to giving his life for us. This Jesus Yeshua stripped himself of all privileges and emptied himself, humbling himself even to death on the cross. He did all of this for us.

He who is above all touched our lives! Let us rejoice and be glad. Let us lift our voices in song and proclaim his love across the nations. Yes, we have pain. Yes, we are hurting. Yes, we experience loss. But Creator Yahweh has experienced these things as well...and he did it for us!

Let us rejoice in the hope he has given us.

Eagle People...Today's reading is Philippians 2:5-8.
Pleya gi. "Go with Blessings."

October 22

Every Knee Shall Bow

Yes warriors! Because of his sacrifice for us, Jesus Yeshua is exalted to the right hand of our Great Chief and Captain. Let us bow our knees to our Creator now.

There is coming a day when all who believe in the name of Jesus Yeshua will bow down before him. All who do not believe will bow down to him. All who think they have a complaint against Him, will voice no complaint when they see Him for who He is. Every tongue will confess He is Lord. All who think they do not believe in Him, will bow in reverence before His throne. Not because they are made to bow, but because His glory demands nothing less.

This is the ONE we serve! Let us do so with humble hearts and great joy!

Eagle People...Today's reading is Philippians 2:9-11.
Pleya gi. "Go with Blessings."

October 23

Eternal Delight

We have all known the dark hour of the soul when Jesus Yeshua seems very far away, especially when he has allowed something precious to be taken away from us. But know this warriors, he is faithful and trustworthy and completely and utterly good. He will restore whatever is lost many times over.

Today is not his only day to work. Neither is tomorrow or next week or even next year. He works beyond our death. Do not believe the lie that the grave opens on nothing but infinite darkness and eternal silence. For those who have committed their way to Creator Yahweh and give him all their length of days, it opens on eternal delight.

Our bodies may fail us, our hearts may deceive us, but restoration is one of his many great promises. Not one Word has failed of all the good promises he gave to our ancestors. He will never leave us or forsake us. He will fulfill all his promises to us, and not a moment too late. Let our hearts be fully committed to our Great Chief and Captain.

Eagle People...Today's reading is 1 Kings 8:56-61.
Pleya gi. "Go with Blessings."

October 24

A Rich Inheritance

Warriors, let us pray for one another. Let us keep asking our Great Chief and Captain to give us the Spirit of wisdom, revelation and insight so that we can know him better. Let us also pray that the eyes of our hearts will be enlightened so that we will know the hope to which Creator Yahweh has called us. We have a rich inheritance.

Let us pray that we will understand the incomparably great power that Creator Yahweh has given us who believe. This power is like the working of his mighty strength, the same strength he exerted when He raised Jesus Yeshua from the dead and seated him in the heavenly realms.

Our Great Chief and Captain is far above all rule and authority, power and dominion, not only in this present age but also in the one to come. This Holy Spirit power lives in us! We are a chosen people! We are a loved people! Let us be thankful and love one another as Creator Yahweh loves us. Never grow tired of reminding each other of these things. It is a good way of walking in Beauty.

Eagle People...Today's reading is Ephesians 1:15-21.
Pleya gi. "Go with Blessings."

October 25

Trust Him With Your Tomorrows

Warriors, you can trust all laws of our Great Chief and Captain. His laws are perfect, reviving the soul. His statutes are trustworthy making wise the simple. In the heavens he has pitched a tent for the sun. Every day it is like a bridegroom coming out of his tent, ready to meet his bride. It is like a great champion ready and rejoicing to run his course, knowing he is ready to do so. The sun rises at one end of the heavens and makes its circuit to the other; nothing is hidden from its heat.

This is just one of the many wonders found in the heavens Creator Yahweh created. The heavens put on a marvelous display day after day; their splendor is seen night after night. Seasons are counted upon these wonders; seas are navigated. These laws and ordinances of our Great Chief and Captain are sure and always right.

He is not slack in keeping his promise. Let us trust him with our tomorrows. He will restore our thirsty, tired souls.

Eagle People...Today's reading is Psalm 19:4-7.
Pleya gi. "Go with Blessings."

October 26

Evidence in the Wind

Our people have always known that Creator existed. Our ancestors saw his evidence in the wind carrying his life-giving breath. Our people numbered their days and found direction by the stars in the sky and the rocks on the earth. They witnessed Creator's delight over the birth of a fawn and the flight of an eagle. It has been this way since the creation of the world.

Our hearts jump at the witness of his power! The invisible nature of the Great Spirit, and his attributes, his eternal power and divinity, have been made known and clearly discernible in and through the things that he has created.

We have been given a choice to either recognize Creator as God and honor and glorify him as our Great Chief and Captain... or repress and hinder the truth and make it inoperative. Answer for yourselves. Does your heart not tell you which choice is the way of walking in Beauty?

The days are short warriors! Choose this day whom you will serve! Then do it with all your heart, with all your soul, with all your mind, and with all your strength. Walk in Spirit power as never before.

Eagle People...Today's reading is Romans 1:19-20.
Pleya gi. "Go with Blessings."

October 27

The Only Wise One

It is good to honor Creator's creation. To respect beauty and cleanse the land, but be careful warriors. It is also important to give honor and glory to our Great Chief and Captain above all.

We must be careful to not become futile and godless in our thinking with imaginings and foolish reasoning. Let us not claim to be wise when Creator Yahweh alone is wise. Let us not exchange the glory and majesty and excellence of the immortal God for images of his created birds and beasts and reptiles. If we do, our Great Chief and Captain will give us up to the lusts of our own hearts.

Let us be careful to not exchange the truth of Creator Yahweh for a lie and worship and serve created things rather than the Creator. Instead, let us bless Creator Yahweh forever and let our lips never cease in giving him praise! Then his wisdom will fill our hearts and we will walk in Spirit power.

Eagle People … Today's reading is Romans 1:21-25.
Pleya gi. "Go with Blessings."

October 28

Look at Your Own Heart

Warriors, may it never be said of us that we did not see fit to acknowledge Creator Yahweh or approve of Him or consider Him worth the knowing!

When people reach this state, Our Great Chief and Captain gives them over to their base and condemned mind until they are saturated with every kind of unrighteousness and wrong doing. Let us pray for those we see heading down this path. Let us ask Creator Yahweh to not let go of our loved ones, to not give them over to their senseless grasping, but to keep wooing them by Spirit power from the jaws of death. Let us also look at our own hearts, asking the Holy Spirit to wash them clean, and let us make sure we have repented daily from any wrong doing that Spirit power has made us aware of. Let us acknowledge our Creator and dive into the *Sacred Writings* and get to know him more and more with each passing day!

It is Creator Yahweh's kindness that draws us to repentance. Let us show his kindness to one another.

Eagle People...Today's reading is Romans 1:26-2:5.
Pleya gi. "Go with Blessings."

October 29

Lies From The Enemy

Our people have seen many witnesses who have blasphemed and spoken wrongly of the name of Creator Yahweh. They burdened our people with laws and decrees that never came from the mouth of our Great Chief and Captain. They have tried to make us act and look like themselves, not realizing that they had fallen far from the image of Holiness portrayed by Jesus Yeshua.

Do not let these people steal your grace! Their words about Creator Yahweh are often no more than lies from our enemy, that evil trickster. Do not mistake their lies for the truth found in the *Sacred Writings.* Pray for Holy Spirit power to help you discern and understand what is right and true and lovely and just.

We are Spirit people. Let us look to our own hearts. Creator Yahweh created us for a purpose and that purpose includes our traditions and history. Yes, a few things must be put aside, but all that give glory to our Great Chief and Captain remain. Let us dance our prayers with joy and celebrate our uniqueness!

Eagle People...Today's reading is Romans 2:6-29.
Pleya gi. "Go with Blessings."

October 30

Have You Not Heard?

Do you not know, warriors? Have you not heard? Has it not been told you from the beginning? Didn't our ancestors tell us that Creator formed the earth?

Creator Yahweh sits enthroned above the circle of the earth, and its people are like grasshoppers. He is the One who stretched out the heavens like a great canopy. He is the One who brings out the starry host one by one and calls them each by name. Because of his great power and mighty strength, not one of them is missing. Do you not know, warriors? Have you not heard? Our Great Chief and Captain is the everlasting God, the Creator of the ends of the earth! This is the one we serve. Let us do so with all our strength and joy!

Eagle People...Today's reading is Isaiah 40: 21-28.
Pleya gi. "Go with Blessings."

October 31

Beyond Us!

Know this, warriors! Creator Yahweh is The Everlasting God and he will never grow faint or weary. No one can fathom or search out his understanding. It is beyond us. Yet, he gives power to the faint and strength to the weary. Even young warriors grow tired and weary, and young men stumble and fall exhausted.

But those warriors who hope in Creator Yahweh, who expect and look for our Great Chief and Captain, will renew their strength and power!

We shall rise on wings as eagles and mount up close to Creator Yahweh! We will run and not grow weary. We will walk and not faint! Our Great Chief and Captain chose us to be his servants! Do not fear, for he is always with us. Listen for his voice in the quiet nights and know his touch throughout each day.

Eagle People...Today's reading is
Isaiah 40: 28-31 & 41:9-10.
Pleya gi. "Go with Blessings."

Ralph Medina

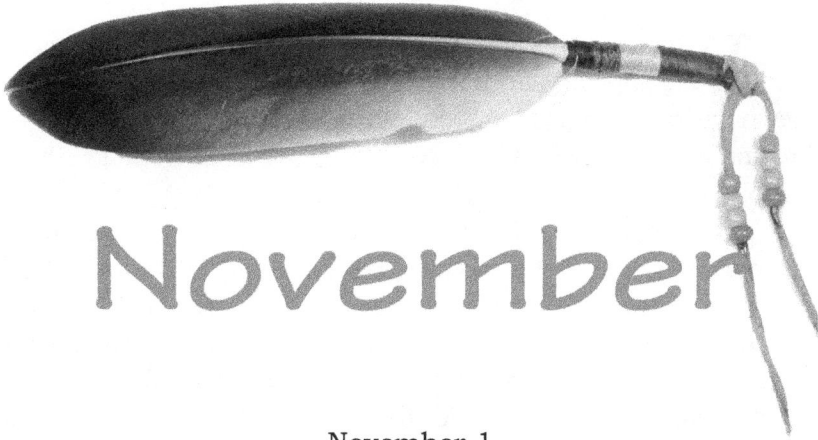

November

November 1

Poison to Our Souls

Warriors, we have long known the difference between right and wrong. We feel good about ourselves when we do what is right, yet when we do something wrong we tend to make excuses. We compare ourselves with someone else who perhaps does a worse wrong and that makes us feel as if our own wrong is not so bad. We must stop ourselves from continuing in such a walk. It is like poison to our souls. For no one will be declared righteous because of observing the law. The law simply made us conscious of our wrong doing.

Our Great Chief and Captain has told us that not one of us is good. Not one. He compares Himself with none other. He is completely good. Compared to him, we all miss the mark. But do not fear, warriors, he has given us a gift! Righteousness through his Son, Jesus Yeshua. He offers complete cleansing, and Holy Spirit power to be able to walk in the way of Beauty.

This gift is ours if we do not turn away. Accept the gift and enjoy your new relationship with Creator Yahweh. Yes, our hearts will often condemn us, but he is greater than our hearts!

Eagle People...Today's reading is Romans 3:1-20.
Pleya gi. "Go with Blessings."

November 2

Blessed Warriors

Warriors, this gift that Creator Yahweh has given us is completely free! We know that when a person works they have wages credited to them, not as a gift but as an obligation. Creator Yahweh's gift is not something we can work for. It is completely free for the one who accepts it.

This is the gift of having our sins forgiven and completely covered. They will never be counted against us again! Jesus Yeshua was delivered over to death for our sins and was raised to life for our justification. If we try to earn this gift then we show that we do not trust Our Great Chief and Captain. But to the one who trusts in Creator Yahweh that he justifies the ungodly, that warrior's faith is credited to him or her as righteousness.

Blessed and happy and to be envied are those warriors of whose sin Creator Yahweh will take no account of or charge against him or her. Let us come with thankful hearts and dance our joy before our Great Chief and Captain.

Eagle People...Today's reading is Romans 4:1-8.
Pleya gi. "Go with Blessings."

November 3

Standing Grace

Warriors, we have been justified through faith, and we have peace with our Great Chief and Captain through Creator Yahweh. It is through him that we have gained access by faith into this grace by which we stand. This grace covers all our wrong doing! This is because we have died to sin.

What shall we say about all this? Shall we go on living our old way of life, doing whatever we want in spite of the consequences? No! We put to death our old lives when we were baptized into the life of Christ. The hallmark of a warrior of Christ is still obedience! But we are no longer obligated to be obedient to the law of Moses. Now we are obedient to the law of Creator Yahweh. And his law is summed up in two commands: Love God and love others. It is a good thing to give our lives to him each day as we step out on the Blessing Way. He is changing us from the inside out.

Eagle People...Today's reading is Romans 5-6:2. *Pleya gi.* "Go with Blessings."

November 4

Free Servants

Warriors, we know that if we continually surrender ourselves to anyone to do his will, then we are the slaves of the one we are surrendering to, whether that be to our enemy, that evil trickster, or in obedience to Creator Yahweh. But we no longer need to surrender ourselves to sin, because our relation to it is broken. We are now alive to God and living in unbroken fellowship with Our Great Chief and Captain in Christ Jesus Yeshua.

Praise our Great Chief and Captain, though we were once slaves of sin and wrong-doing, we have now become obedient with all our hearts to a life of love. This is because we have been set free from sin and have become servants of our Great Chief and Captain.

This does not mean that we never commit a wrong, but it does mean that we are daily being conformed to his divine will in thought, purpose and action. This life is available to us, not only on the Sacred Mountain, but in every aspect of our lives.

Eagle People...Today's reading is Romans 6:11-18. *Pleya gi.* "Go with Blessings."

November 5

Reason to Hope!

Warriors, let us rejoice in the hope of the glory of Our Great Chief and Captain! Creator Yahweh is the LORD our God. He takes hold of our right hand and says, "Do not fear; I will help you. Do not be afraid."

He whispers these words to us even when we feel as if we are no more than a worm, when we are small and insignificant in comparison to our enemies, when we walk dark paths with little light to brighten our way. His breath blows across the mountains and valleys and enters our souls, giving hope where all was lost. It is then, in our darkest of dark places, that our Great Chief and Captain declares that he will help us. We have reason to hope and reason to rejoice. Our Redeemer is Creator Yahweh and we know that he lives, not only in the air that we breathe but also within our very souls.

Eagle People...Today's reading is Isaiah 41:13-16.
Pleya gi. "Go with Blessings."

November 6

Healing of The Brokenhearted

This is what Our Great Chief and Captain says, he who created the heavens and stretched them forth, he who spread out the earth and all that comes out of it, he who gives breath to the people of the earth and Holy Spirit to those who walk in it: "I, Creator Yahweh, have called you in righteousness; I will take hold of your hand. I will keep you and will make you to be a covenant for the people and a light for the Gentiles, to open eyes that are blind, to free captives from prison and to release from the dungeon those who sit in darkness." Isaiah 42:6-7 (NIV)

Warriors, Jesus Yeshua is our covenant. Yes. It means salvation. Yes it means eternity in his Light. But it also means much more. It means the opening of blinded eyes, the freeing of those who are captive, the healing of the brokenhearted. The former things have come to pass and now our Great Chief and Captain is declaring new things. He has called us for a righteous purpose. Let us sing to Creator Yahweh a new song. Let us dance his praise to the ends of the earth!

Eagle People...Today's reading is Isaiah 42:5-10.
Pleya gi. "Go with Blessings."

November 7

Songs in The Night

Warriors, is there a promise that you feel Creator Yahweh has given you? Have you been waiting a long time to see this promise come to pass? Has he given you glimpses? Have there been times when you felt the fulfilled promise was almost in your hands just to have it snatched away at the last minute? Know this, warriors, our Great Chief and Captain is not slow in keeping his promise to you. He is utterly faithful and the fulfillment will not be a day late. Is there anything too hard or too wonderful for Creator Yahweh?

"Look up at the heavens and see; gaze at the clouds so high above you. If you sin, how does that affect him? If your sins are many, what does that do to him? If you are righteous, what do you give to him, or what does he receive from your hand? Your wickedness affects only a human like yourself, and your righteousness only the sons and daughters of men." Job 35:5-8 (NIV)

Let us cry out to Creator Yahweh saying, "Where is God my Maker, who gives songs of rejoicing in the night, who teaches more to us than to the beasts of the earth and makes us wiser than the birds of the air?" Job 35:10-11 (NIV)

Ascribing such glory to our Great Chief and Captain will strengthen our hearts. He delivers the afflicted from their affliction and opens our ears to hear his voice. Be still, warriors, and listen carefully.

Eagle People...Today's reading is
Genesis 18:10-14 & Job 35:1-11.
Pleya gi. "Go with Blessings."

November 8

A Far-Seeing Place

Warriors let us ascribe justice to Creator Yahweh, our Maker! He is wooing us from the jaws of distress to a spacious, far-seeing place, to the comfort of a banquet table laden with all the best food. This is one of the promises we have to look forward to that will not be a day late.

While we are waiting for the fulfillment of the promise, let us be careful that no one entices us with riches. Such a lifestyle may turn us aside from walking in beauty. And when affliction comes, let us beware of turning to evil. Instead, let us climb the Sacred Mountain, whether in Spirit or in body, and seek the face of Creator Yahweh.

How magnificent is our Great Chief and Captain—beyond our understanding! The number of his years is past finding out. We can trust such a One as this. Let us take shelter in the shadow of his wings.

Eagle People...Today's reading is Job 35:12-26.
Pleya gi. "Go with Blessings."

November 9

Be Still & Know

Warriors, are you broken and battle weary? Do not forget that we are a spiritual people. We need the power of stillness to feed our souls. Creator Yahweh has made us this way, so that we will spend time to get to know him. This is why we climb the Sacred Mountain, whether in body or in Spirit, to get alone with him and hear his voice above all others. There is only one way to know God and that is to "Be still, and know."

It is when we stop focusing on ourselves that we discover the peace that transcends all understanding. Lift your eyes to the hills. Lift your hearts to the heavens. In these times of solitude we learn the power of silence, the incredible calm before the thundering storm. When we return to our Great Chief and Captain and when we rest in him, we find salvation. In quietness and trust we find our strength.

Weary warrior, Creator Yahweh longs to be gracious to you; he rises to show you compassion. Blessed are all who wait for him!

Eagle People...Today's reading is Isaiah 30:15-18.
Pleya gi. "Go with Blessings."

November 10

Sacred Communion

Warriors, when was the last time you caught a glimpse of the Spiritual realm? Have you climbed the Sacred Mountain, whether in Spirit or in body, and sat at the feet of our Great Chief and Captain? Have you tasted of the sweet communion Creator Yahweh offers for all who believe? It is in this place of holy communion that we feel a surging wave of joy and hope.

All warriors who claim to follow the Jesus Way must set aside special times and places for quiet communion with our Great Chief and Captain. King David, in the *Sacred Writings,* looked to the hills whenever he was in the valley. He climbed those hills in Spirit whenever he needed wise council. Daniel, who was held captive, set aside a spiritual place in his small room in order to commune with God. Others could see Daniel and yet he blocked everything out in order to gain strength from his Great Chief and Captain.

We as a spiritual people must return to a life of quietness, prayer, and *Sacred Writings.* Like David and Daniel, we need to find these places in our everyday lives, making room and time for Creator Yahweh. When we return to a life of spiritual visions, our Great Chief and Captain will once again take us to the mountaintop where we will receive glimpses of heaven. And those glimpses are what we need, warriors, in order to stand firm like good dog soldiers.

Eagle People...Today's reading is Ephesians 2:1-7.
Pleya gi. "Go with Blessings."

November 11

Incomparable Riches

There was a time, warriors, when we were dead to Holy Spirit power. This is the way we formerly walked on a path that appeared to be smooth but led only into darkness. We were tricked by the ruler of the kingdom of the air. This is the trickster spirit who is alive in all who are disobedient to our Great Chief and Captain.

Every one of us once lived among the disobedient at one time, gratifying the cravings of our sinful nature and following its desires and thoughts. We were careless, rebellious and unbelieving, going against the purposes of our Great Chief and Captain.

Some of us ended up following the alcohol way, some of us drank our way into oblivion and yet others of us were eaten alive by anger, allowing bitterness to color every aspect of our lives, destroying our children and loved ones in the process. We were by nature children of God's wrath and deserving of nothing good.

But our Great Chief and Captain, so incredibly rich in mercy and overflowing with love, reached out to us when we were on that dark path and made us alive in Christ Jesus Yeshua! He birthed us into Spirit power and raised us up with Jesus Yeshua and seated us there with him in the heavenly realms. He did all this in order to demonstrate the incomparable, immeasurable and limitless riches of his free grace given through belief in his son. This unearned and unmerited favor is expressed in his kindness and goodness of heart toward us in Christ Jesus Yeshua.

Let us remain in Spirit power, warriors, even if it means re-climbing the Sacred Mountain, whether in Spirit or in body. Let us leave the clamor and noise of a crazy-making world and tune in to the voice of Creator Yahweh.

Eagle People...Today's reading is Luke 9:28-35.
Pleya gi. "Go with Blessings."

November 12

Examine Your Heart

Warriors, do you want to claim all the fullness of Creator Yahweh's promises? Do you long to see all the possibilities come to pass? Light the sage and let its pleasing aroma fall over your body, cleansing you from head to toe, then sing your prayers as never before. Pray through each aspect of your circumstances. Lift each moment to our Great Chief and Captain! Then ask for his Spirit power as you fully examine your heart. Let him show you why he has allowed these circumstances to enter your life.

Sometimes he allows pain in order for us to see a deep need that we wouldn't otherwise, whether for ourselves or for someone else. Other times he allows pain in order to draw us into a deeper relationship with him that we would not have pursued otherwise.

Creator Yahweh is able to do immeasurably more than all we ask or imagine, according to his power that is at work within us. Examine your heart and trust him, warriors, he is faithful.

Eagle People...Today's reading is Ephesians 3:20-21.
Pleya gi. "Go with Blessings."

<u>November 13</u>

Unity of The Spirit

Warriors, walk in a manner worthy of the calling you have received. Creator Yahweh has designed us to live in unity as one body and one Spirit, just as we have been called into one hope and one bond of peace. Be strong! Take courage. And make every effort to keep this unity of the Holy Spirit.

The world tells us to think about ourselves, but our Great Chief and Captain tells us to think of others as better than ourselves. The world tells us to love ourselves, but our Great Chief and Captain tells us to love Him and to love others. Let us be humble and gentle. Let us be patient, bearing with one another in love. This does not mean we are any less the warrior. We are more so! We guard the harmony and unity of the Spirit by coming against our enemy, that evil trickster, who tries to divide and separate us.

Eagle People...Today's reading is Ephesians 4:1-4.
Pleya gi. "Go with Blessings."

<u>November 14</u>

Soul Care

Warriors, because we are a spiritual people it is important that we take care of our souls. When we began to walk the Jesus Way we were taught to put off our old self with its deceitful and corrupted desires. Creator Yahweh clothed us with a new robe of righteousness. We were made new in the attitude of our minds, and we became sensitive to the ways of our Great Chief and Captain. Our old selves had a continual lust that was never satisfied. Our new selves are led by Holy Spirit power into freedom.

It is for freedom that Christ Jesus Yeshua set us free, so why do we allow ourselves to fall back into a yoke of slavery? Do not give our enemy, that evil trickster, a foothold. Do not conform to the patterns of this world. Let us renew our minds by diving into the depths of the *Sacred Writings* and allowing our Great Chief and Captain to lead us along the way of grace. This is how we take care of our souls and remain a spiritual people.

Eagle People…Today's reading is Ephesians 4:17-24.
Pleya gi. "Go with Blessings."

November 15

Fire & Water

Warriors, do not forget that it is Creator Yahweh who has created us. He formed us while we were yet in the womb. It is he who tells us that he has redeemed us. He has called us by name! He has promised that when we pass through the waters, he will be with us. When we pass through fast moving rivers, they will not sweep over us. When we walk through the fire, we will not be burned. Flames will not set us ablaze! Our enemy, that evil trickster, might hurt our bodies but he can never touch our souls. For our Great Chief and Captain is always with us. Creator Yahweh, the Holy One over all the earth, is our Savior.

We are precious and honored in his sight. So do not be afraid, warriors. Take courage! Creator Yahweh loves us! Before him no god was formed and there will be none after him. Apart from him there is no Savior. He has revealed and saved and proclaimed. Let us respond to his great love by dancing before him and lifting our voices in praise! Yahweh. Yahweh. Yahweh. Holy is his name.

Eagle People…Today's reading is Isaiah 43:1-13.
Pleya gi. "Go with Blessings."

November 16

Chosen & Dearly Loved

Warriors, it is important that we make it our goal to be imitators of our Great Chief and Captain. Not as clones who have no choice, but as those who have been chosen as dearly loved children.

We are a family. Let us not allow any unwholesome talk to come out of our mouths, but only what is helpful for building others up according to their needs. If we treat others in this way, we will be honoring our traditions and ancestors as well as honoring our Great Chief and Captain. Let us think how we can encourage others.

If someone offends us, then let us ask Creator Yahweh to fill us with Spirit power to be able to see that person in the way he sees them, for he sees their hearts. Let us ask him to show us our brother and sister's true heart need.

Many times we will need to ask for forgiveness for our anger and unwholesome thoughts. Sometimes we will need to ask the person for forgiveness. Always we must ask our Great Chief and Captain to help us forgive those who have wronged us. This one thing will help us to stay moving forward on the Beauty Way.

Eagle People...Today's reading is Ephesians 4:29-5:2.
Pleya gi. "Go with Blessings."

November 17

Born of Light

Warriors, we were once children of darkness. Now we are children of light. So let us cast off the ways of darkness and walk as children of Light. Let us be warriors who fight against evil and are Native-born to the Light. When we do this we will produce fruit that is born of the Light. This is Holy Spirit fruit in every form of goodness, uprightness of heart and trueness of life.

Let us always be learning what is pleasing to our Great Chief and Captain and take no part in deeds of darkness. Let us, instead, live a life that shows such a contrast that it exposes the deeds of darkness and invites others to wake from their dead ways and walk in the Light.

We can only do this by Holy Spirit power. Such power shines the light of Creator Yahweh down upon us so that we can see the way to walk. Let us wake from our dead ways and purpose to live a life worthy of the calling of our Great Chief and Captain. With each sunrise let us ask for Holy Spirit power to show us the way. Where everything is visible and clear, there is Light.

Eagle People...Today's reading is Ephesians 5:3-13.
Pleya gi. "Go with Blessings."

November 18

Morning Renewal

Sometimes, warriors, no matter how hard we try not to we fall back into the old way of walking in darkness. Perhaps it's because of hurt feelings or an offense that we cannot let go of. Perhaps we have been wronged in a very real way. Whatever the cause, it sends us reeling back into a position of self-defense against someone other than our real enemy, that evil trickster.

When this happens, it is good to remember that our enemy is the father of lies and that without Holy Spirit power we will believe every lie he tells us. We believe the lie that we need to defend ourselves when in truth our Great Chief and Captain is our defense. The Sword is in the Captain's hand! We believe the lie that we are not loved when in truth Creator Yahweh loves us with pure, faithful, unending love enough to call us his brothers and sisters, not just in word, but in truth and through his blood! We believe the lie that we deserve something better when in truth we deserve nothing but punishment. Yet we do not receive punishment because Creator Yahweh stood in our place and took our punishment on himself.

It is because of Creator Yahweh's great mercy that we are renewed every morning. Take time to sit at his feet. Bask in his love and dwell on his words. These things will bring you back into truth and Holy Spirit power so that you can again walk the Beauty Way. When we are walking in Beauty we will take no offense but choose to approve the good. We will believe in the power of forgiveness and restoration and let our Great Chief and Captain act as the rightful judge. When we spend time with Creator Yahweh we will believe the truth and discard the lie.

Eagle People...Today's reading is Lamentations 3:19-26.
Pleya gi. "Go with Blessings."

November 19

Discipline of Waiting

Warriors, it takes years of training to learn the discipline of waiting. If you are currently in that space where you are being forced to wait rest assured that Creator Yahweh is still in control. While you are waiting, indecision may come. Confusion may hinder your peace. You may have no idea which direction to take, but do not allow yourself to be overcome with despair.

This is a time to be still. Do not rush ahead. Do not cower in fear. Our Great Chief and Captain will give the order to move at just the right time. Nations may be in uproar. Kingdoms may fall. But Creator Yahweh will not be a day late. Be still and know that he is God. He will be exalted in the heavens. He will be exalted in the earth.

Creator Yahweh lives inside us. Everywhere he dwells is a safe place.

Eagle People...Today's reading is Psalm 46.
Pleya gi. "Go with Blessings."

November 20

Reverent Fear

Do not forget, Warriors, that the Law found in the *Sacred Writings* is perfect. Through it, our tired, thirsty souls are revived and restored. We are brought back to life! We can trust the testimony of our Great Chief and Captain. It is sure, making wise the simple. His teachings for personal conduct are completely right. When we follow them our heart is full of rejoicing!

It is good to hold reverent fear when we read the precepts of our Great Chief and Captain. Such holy fear makes us clean and endures forever. The ordinances decreed by Creator Yahweh are always completely right. By following them we live a more honest life.

The laws and precepts of our Great Chief and Captain warn us when we are about to make a choice that will leave us walking the Sorrow Way. They remind us of what is good and right and true and just. They give light to all our dark places and reveal a future and a hope.

We would do well to desire these things more than riches and prosperity for they will bring true sweetness into our lives.

Eagle People...Today's reading is Psalm 19:7-11.
Pleya gi. "Go with Blessings."

November 21

Care For One Another

Warriors, do not forget that fasting and ritual is more than about food and rules. The *Sacred Writings* tell us what our Great Chief and Captain truly wants of us...to loose the chains of injustice and untie the cords of those in bondage. He desires to see the oppressed go free and that we break every yoke that holds his people back.

Let us care for one another. Let us share our food with the hungry and provide shelter for those in need. Let us not turn away our own flesh and blood! This is the desire of Creator Yahweh to see us loving him and loving others, not just in word, but in action and in truth. When we do these things our Light will break forth like the dawn and healing and restoration will quickly take place.

Eagle People...Today's reading is Isaiah 58:6-8.
Pleya gi. "Go with Blessings."

November 22

Come into The Light!

Creator Yahweh is the Light and in him is no darkness at all. Let us purpose to do nothing that will separate us from his great Light. Let us be very careful then, how we live—not as unwise but as wise, making the most of every opportunity. If we live in the Light we will have nothing to do will shameful and evil practices that will tear our families apart and rob our souls of beauty.

Warriors, we have long known that walking the alcohol way is not a good thing. It is one of the things that keeps us in the darkness. We may tell ourselves that we can handle it, that the demons of alcohol will not grab us but in our hearts we know the truth. There is no light or beauty in hiding our souls in such a way. Let us come into the Light!

Let us look to our Great Chief and Captain and climb the Sacred Mountain, whether in body or in Spirit, and discover his unique purpose for us. If we seek him in this, he will lead us, one step at a time, until at last we know we have entered into the Beauty Way.

Eagle People...Today's reading is Ephesians 5:15-16.
Pleya gi. "Go with Blessings."

November 23

What is Right & Just

Warriors, be careful that whatever you do is done on the foundation of righteousness and never by injustice. Do what is right and just. Never give up defending the cause of the poor and needy.

This is what it means to know Creator Yahweh. We should not love with word and with tongue but with action and in deed and sincerity. If you see a brother or sister in need do what you can to help. By this we will come to know and understand that we are of the Truth.

Do not be surprised, brothers and sisters, when the world hates you. We have full assurance that we have passed from death to Life, because we love our bothers and sisters. This love comes from the Holy Spirit living in us! Anyone who does not love remains, is held, and kept continually in spiritual death. Anyone who hates his brother or sister is at heart a murderer. No murderer has eternal life abiding in him.

Let us love one another. If you cannot get beyond hate, then climb the Sacred Mountain, whether in body or in Spirit, and ask Creator Yahweh for his love to work through you. He will set your heart at rest in his presence.

Eagle People...Today's reading is
Jeremiah 22: 15-17 & 1 John 3:11-15.
Pleya gi. "Go with Blessings."

November 24

Shun False Hope

Warriors, Let us make sure we know the *Sacred Writings* well enough so that we can tell the difference between the truth and a lie. Not every spirit that speaks is from our Great Chief and Captain. Some prophets will fill us with false hopes, speaking visions from their own minds, not from the mouth of Creator Yahweh. They will tell us everything we long to hear, but they are living a lie.

Dreams and visions from Creator Yahweh will always align with the words in his *Sacred Writings*. They will strengthen the hands of the poor and needy and give real hope to those in despair. They will not promise what cannot be attained.

Let us speak about what we know and what we have seen. Let us proclaim Words of Life, the Eternal Life, Jesus Yeshua who was with the Father and has appeared to our ancestors. May we be a people who speak faithfully the words of our Great Chief and Captain. In this way we will give life to one another and walk in Light.

Eagle People...Today's reading is
Jeremiah 23:13-21 & 1 John 1:1-7.
Pleya gi. "Go with Blessings."

November 25

Stand in Council

Do not forget warriors, that Creator Yahweh fills heaven and earth. There is no place near or far that he does not see. There is no secret place that he cannot find us. Before a word was ever on our tongues, he knew us; he called us by name.

Let us stand in the council of our Great Chief and Captain, then we will be able to proclaim his words to our people and help turn them from walking the Sorrow Way. His words are like a fire, burning in our hearts. His promises give us a hope and a future. There is coming a day when he will build us up and not tear us down; he will plant us and not uproot us. He is giving us a heart to know him as our Great Chief and Captain.

Take hope warriors! Creator Yahweh is preparing a place for us, a land free and spacious, for we are his people and the sheep of his pasture.

Eagle People...Today's reading is
Jeremiah 23:22-29 & 24:4-7.
Pleya gi. "Go with Blessings."

November 26

True Restoration

We have much to be thankful for warriors. Creator Yahweh has called us by name! Our Maker is like a husband to us, keeping our house together. Let us be thankful for his unfailing love that can never be shaken, for his everlasting kindness and compassion, and for his covenant of peace that will never be removed. Our Great Chief and Captain will enlarge our tents and strengthen our stakes, spreading us out to the right and to the left. Our descendants will settle throughout the earth.

Let us praise the name of Creator Yahweh because he has taken away our fear and has filled us with Spirit power so that we will forget the shame of our youth. He has called us back to himself and has promised true restoration for those who acknowledge him in word and Spirit.

"Sing, O barren woman, you who never bore a child; burst into song, shout for joy, you who were never in labor; because more are the children of the desolate woman than of her who has a husband. Isaiah 54:1 (NIV)

Our Great Chief and Captain is our Redeemer; he is called the God of all the earth.

Eagle People...Today's reading is Isaiah 54.
Pleya gi. "Go with Blessings."

November 27

Sanctuary of The Stars

Warriors take time to seek Creator Yahweh while he may be found; call upon him while he is near. Things will not always be as they are now. Let the wicked person forsake walking the wicked way and let the evil person give up and exchange their evil thoughts. Let us all turn to our Great Chief and Captain for he will have mercy on us. Let us turn to our God, for he will freely pardon.

Warriors, I pray that Creator Yahweh will answer you whenever you are in distress. Lift your voice to him, for his very name offers you protection. Our Great Chief and Captain will send you help from the sanctuary of the stars and grant you all the support you need. He will not forget the sweet fragrance of your offerings. I pray that he will give you all the desires of your heart and make all your plans succeed.

Eagle People...Today's reading is Isaiah 56:6-7.
Pleya gi. "Go with Blessings."

November 28

Words of Life!

Do not forget warriors, as far as the heavens are above the earth, so are the ways of Creator Yahweh higher than our ways and his thoughts far beyond our thoughts. His thoughts are not anything like our thoughts. Rain pours from the clouds and snow covers the earth, and neither return to heaven without first watering the earth and making it bud and spring to life so that it yields seed for the sower and nourishment for the gatherer.

So it is with the words found in the *Sacred Writings,* which are the very words of our Great Chief and Captain. His words will accomplish his desires and will achieve the purposes for which he sent it. His words hold life for us! By them we are warned from walking the Sorrow Way. By them we see the way ahead one step at a time. By them we find nourishment for our souls. Trust in the thoughts and the words and the promises of Creator Yahweh. They will accomplish great things in the lives of warriors who heed them.

Eagle People...Today's reading is Isaiah 58:8-11.
Pleya gi. "Go with Blessings."

November 29

Salvation is Close at Hand!

Take heart warriors! There is coming a day when we will go out with joy and be led forth in peace. The mountains and the hills will break forth into singing before you. All the trees of the field will clap their hands. On this great day the briars and thorn brush will cease to grow and great forests will stretch before us. See

Isaiah 55:12-13 (NIV). While we are waiting for this glorious day, let us maintain justice and do what is right. For this day could come at any moment, in the twinkling of an eye, everything can change.

Creator Yahweh's salvation is close at hand! His righteousness will soon be revealed. Blessed are the warriors who hold fast to this promise and keep their hands from doing any evil.

Eagle People...Today's reading is Isaiah 56:1-2.
Pleya gi. "Go with Blessings."

November 30

Pass Down The Old Stories

Remember warriors, to be very careful how you live, not as unwise but as wise, making the most of every opportunity. Your life on this earth road is short, not much more than a vapor. Creator Yahweh has placed you here for a unique purpose. Make it your goal to find out what that purpose is and to walk in it in Holy Spirit power.

Do not get drunk on wine, but be filled with the Holy Spirit! Such a filling of Holy Spirit will make you dance for joy. Speak to one another with traditional songs and new songs. Let the faithfulness of our Great Chief and Captain be made known. Pass down the old stories and let your story be heard by your children. Sing and make music in your heart to Creator Yahweh, always giving thanks for everything. And while you do these things, be sure to submit to one another in love, for love covers over a multitude of wrong doing.

Eagle People...Today's reading is Ephesians 5:15-21.
Pleya gi. "Go with Blessings."

Richard Twiss

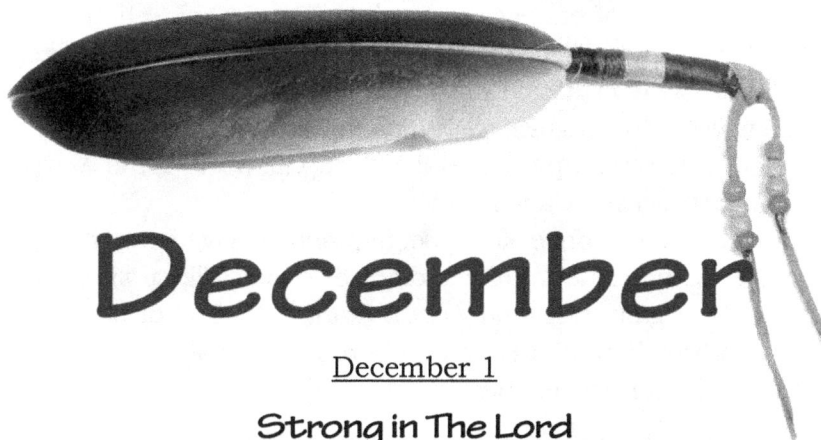

December

Strong in The Lord

Warriors! "Be strong in the Lord and in his mighty power! Put on the full armor of *our Great Chief and Captain* so that you can take your stand against the devil's schemes. For our fight is not against flesh and blood. It is against the rulers, against the authorities, against the powers of this dark world and against the spiritual forces of evil in the heavenly realms." Ephesians 6:10-12 (NIV)

Sometimes it is good to remember past wrongs so that the evil parts of history will not be repeated, but be careful! Do not allow bitterness to overtake you or you will lose your joy and any hope of restoration. Approve the good and be thankful at all times, for there is much to be thankful for. And continue to fight your battles in the spiritual realm where true restoration takes place.

Eagle People...Today's reading is Ephesians 6:10-12.
Pleya gi. "Go with Blessings."

December 2

Stand Your Ground

Warriors, have you put on your full armor? It is important that we have the belt of truth buckled around our waists and the breastplate of righteousness in place. Righteousness is the free gift offered by Jesus Yeshua, and truth is found in the *Sacred Writings* given to us by our Great Chief and Captain.

Our moccasins must be fitted with the readiness that comes from the gospel of peace given to us by Creator Yahweh and our headdress is the protection of his salvation that is also given freely to all warriors who trust in him. We must also pick up the shield of faith, which will extinguish all the flaming arrows of the evil trickster. Then we must pick up the Sword of the Spirit, which is the Word of our Great Chief and Captain.

Once we have done all this, let us stand firm with everything in place. Then when the day of evil comes, as it soon will, we will be able to stand our ground and pray in the Spirit with all kinds of prayers and requests. With all this in mind, we must be alert and always keep praying for one another.

Eagle People...Today's reading is Ephesians 6:13-18.
Pleya gi. "Go with Blessings."

December 3

Joy Comes in The Morning

Many mighty warriors have fallen and been laid to rest. We cry and we mourn because of our great loss, and that is an honorable thing, but do we ponder this in our hearts...that merciful and faithful warriors are taken away to escape the evil that is coming our way. Those who walk with Creator Yahweh leave the cares and troubles of this world and enter into peace when they take their last breath. They enter through heaven's gate hearing the words, "Well done, good and faithful servant."

This is because our Great Chief and Captain lives in a high and lofty place far above the stars; He inhabits eternity and his name is Holy. Without him was nothing made that was made. He is the Creator of all things. But he also lives within our hearts. He is with the lowly and contrite in heart. He will revive the spirits of warriors who feel faint and are nearly consumed. He also revives the hearts of warriors who are bruised with sorrow because of a mountain of wrongs. He will guide us and restore peace and comfort to us, creating praise on the lips of those who now mourn.

Stand firm, mighty warriors. We are called as a unique people to serve Creator Yahweh with all our heart and strength. Sorrow follows us through the night but joy comes in the morning.

Eagle People...Today's reading is Isaiah 57:1-16.
Pleya gi. "Go with Blessings."

December 4

Light of Life

W arriors, let us do away with the yoke of oppression, with the pointing finger and malicious talk. Let us, instead, encourage one another and stir up the gifts Creator Yahweh has given us. Let us spend ourselves on behalf of the hungry and strive to satisfy the needs of the oppressed. By doing these things our Light will rise in the darkness so that even the night will shine like noonday.

Creator Yahweh, Jesus Yeshua, is the Light of the world. Warriors who follow him will never walk in darkness. Instead, they will shine with the Light of life, because they walk in Holy Spirit power.

This is the verdict: Light has come into the world, but men and women loved darkness instead of light because their deeds were evil. Everyone who does evil hates the light, and will not come into the light for fear that his deeds will be exposed. But whoever lives by the truth comes into the light so that it may be seen plainly that whatever they have done has been done through our Great Chief and Captain." John 3:19-21 (NIV)

Eagle People ... Today's reading is
Isaiah 58:9-12 & John 8:12 & 3:19-21.
Pleya gi. "Go with Blessings."

December 5

Repairer of Broken Walls

W arriors, our Great Chief and Captain will guide us always! He will satisfy our needs in a sun-scorched land. He will strengthen our frame and we will be like a well-watered garden, like a spring whose waters never fail. Call on Creator Yahweh. He is our help and our rear guard. He will hear our cry for help and will say, "Here I Am." The day is coming when we will rebuild the ancient ruins and will raise up the age-old foundations. We will be called

Repairer of Broken Walls and Restorer of Streets with Dwellings. Let us find joy in Creator Yahweh for his arm is not too short to save, nor his ear too dull to hear.

It is our own wrong doing that stands in the way, yet because of his great mercy Jesus Yeshua has broken down every wall, even the wall of our wrong doing. Delight yourself in our Great Chief and Captain and he will make you to ride on the high places of the earth. He will satisfy our hunger with good things. Call upon Creator Yahweh. He will answer. He is our peace.

Eagle People…Today's reading is
Isaiah 58:9-14 & 59:1-2.
Pleya gi. "Go with Blessings."

December 6

The Year of Release

Warriors do not forget that the Spirit of Creator Yahweh, the Sovereign Lord, is upon us! Because we have given ourselves to him, he has anointed us to preach good news to the poor. We can preach the good news that he will bind up the brokenhearted. Let us proclaim freedom for the captives!

If we lay our lives at his feet and claim him as our Great Chief and Captain, then we can trust him! This can be the year of release for those whose hearts are held captive by fear and worry. This can be the year we realize our worth in him. This is the year we proclaim Creator Yahweh's favor!

Walk in newness warriors. Do not believe the lies of our enemy, that evil trickster. Do not hold onto old grudges or past hurts. Cast all your cares on your faithful Creator and serve him with all your heart, soul, mind and strength. This is the way to walk in joy. This is the way of walking in Beauty.

Some trust in chariots and some in horses, but we trust in the name of Creator Yahweh. Let us rise and stand firm.

Eagle People…Today's reading is Isaiah 61:1-2.
Pleya gi. "Go with Blessings."

December 7

Regalia of Praise

Do you feel alone warriors? Do not forget that Creator Yahweh stands with open arms to comfort all who mourn. Yes. We suffer loss. Yes. We endure pain. He knows. He understands. And he promises to bring something good out of these broken places. He will grant joy to those of us who now walk in sorrow. Wait for it. It will not be a day late, though you may think so now.

This is the promise! We will be given the garland of beauty instead of ashes, the oil of joy instead of mourning, and the regalia of praise instead of a heavy and burdened spirit. We will be called oaks of righteousness, lofty, strong, and magnificent trees! We are a planting of Creator Yahweh to glorify our Great Chief and Captain. Keep your faith warriors. Joy is coming.

Eagle People...Today's reading is Isaiah 61:2-3.
Pleya gi. "Go with Blessings."

December 8

An Everlasting Covenant

This is the time of Creator Yahweh's favor. He has clothed us with his righteousness and called us his own. We will rebuild the ancient ruins and restore the places long devastated, even places that have been devastated for generations. The promise is sure that the day is coming when instead of shame our people will receive a double portion, and instead of disgrace we will rejoice in our inheritance. Everlasting joy will be ours!

Our Great Chief and Captain will reward us for simply calling out to him. In faithfulness he has made an everlasting covenant with us, so that our descendants will be known among the nations. All who see will acknowledge that we are a people Creator Yahweh has blessed. This is reason to celebrate. Let us dance with joy!

Eagle People...Today's reading is Isaiah 61:4-9.
Pleya gi. "Go with Blessings."

December 9

The Wolf & The Lamb

Know this warriors, the day is coming when Creator Yahweh will create new heavens and a new earth. The former things will not be remembered, nor will they come to mind. The sound of weeping and of crying will be heard no more. Even now, our Creator takes delight in us!

Yes. The day is coming when we will no longer build houses and others live in them nor will we gather and others eat. We will build houses and dwell in them; we will gather and eat the harvest. Our children will not be doomed to misfortune; for they will be a people blessed by Our Great Chief and Captain. The wolf and the lamb will feed together, and the lion will eat straw like the ox. Even now when we call upon him, Creator Yahweh answers; while we are still speaking, he hears. Take all your sorrows to him.

Eagle People...Today's reading is Isaiah 65:17-25.
Pleya gi. "Go with Blessings."

December 10

Amazing Mystery

Think on this warriors...Heaven is Creator Yahweh's throne and the earth is his footstool. What house can we build for him? Is there any great place where we can contain him? He rides on the wings of the wind and journeys to the birthplace of the sea.

Yet this One...whose hand made all things so that they came into being...dwells in the hearts of those who call out to him. We live and move and have our being in him, yet his Spirit lives within our hearts. Amazing love. Amazing mystery.

The Creator of all things became a man. The Creator of all things took on our guilt and died upon a cross. The Creator of all things rose from the dead, for the grave could not contain him. The Creator of all things calls us by name! Trust him, warriors, even in this season of sorrow. He will restore and rebuild. When you see his day approaching, your heart will rejoice.

Eagle People...Today's reading is Isaiah 66:1-11.
Pleya gi. "Go with Blessings."

December 11

Much Remains

Iknow warriors that many walk the sorrow way at this time. Hearts are broken because of loss. Much has been taken, yet do not forget that much remains. Call out to Creator Yahweh. He will comfort those who mourn and will extend peace like a river.

Yes, we have been hurt. Yes, we want justice. Yet our Great Chief and Captain tells us to feed our enemies and bless those that curse us. Many of our ancestors did this and it freed their souls. The enemy can harm our bodies but they cannot touch our souls if we walk in Holy Spirit power. Think on the good things. Walk the Beauty Way. And hold Creator Yahweh's promises close to your heart.

Eagle People...Today's reading is Isaiah 66:12-13.
Pleya gi. "Go with Blessings."

December 12

Coming with Fire!

Creator Yahweh is coming with fire! His chariots are like a whirlwind. He will bring down his anger with fury, and his rebuke with flames of fire. With fire and with his sword Creator Yahweh will execute judgment upon all humans, and many will be slain by his hand. This is the retribution you are looking for, and it will be done well and good. But know this, warriors, his mercy is very great and he extends love to everyone who calls on his name.

When you see all these things come to pass you will rejoice! You will flourish like grass. The faithful hand of our Great Chief and Captain will be made known to his servants, but his fury will be shown to his foes.

Choose this day whom you will serve. It is not enough to be a warrior, but a warrior must also choose his Captain with wisdom.

Eagle People...Today's reading is Isaiah 66:14-16. *Pleya gi.* "Go with Blessings."

December 13

People of Hope

Ue are in a season of loss where many strong warriors have been lost to us. But let us not be ignorant about those who fall asleep. Let us not grieve like people who have no hope. We believe that Creator Yahweh, Jesus Yeshua, died and rose again, and so we believe that our Great Chief and Captain will bring with Yeshua those who have fallen asleep in him. According to Creator Yahweh's own Word, we who are still alive, who are left till the coming of our Great Chief and Captain, will certainly not precede those who have fallen asleep. For Creator Yahweh, himself, Jesus Yeshua, will come down from heaven, with a loud shout, with the voice of the archangel and with the trumpet call of our Great Chief and Captain!

At that time, "...the dead in Christ will rise first. After that, we who are still alive and are left will be caught up with them in the clouds to meet Creator Yahweh in the air. And so we will be with the LORD forever." 1 Thessalonians 4:17-17 (NIV)

Let us live as people of hope. Let us walk the Beauty Way and celebrate our uniqueness. Let us encourage each other with these words.

Eagle People...Today's reading is 1 Thessalonians 4:13-18. *Pleya gi.* "Go with Blessings."

December 14

Daughters & Sons of Light

Warriors we are daughters and sons of the Light and people of the Day! We do not belong to the night or to the darkness. So then, let us not be like others, who walk as sleeping people. For those who sleep, sleep at night, and those who get drunk, get drunk at night. But let us be alert and self controlled. We do this through Holy Spirit power.

Let us put on faith and love as a breastplate and the hope of salvation as a headdress. For our Great Chief and Captain did not appoint us to suffer wrath but to receive salvation through Creator Yahweh, Jesus Yeshua. He died for us so that whether we are awake or asleep, we may live together with him. Let us encourage one another with these words. Let us speak words of kindness and build each other up. Let us love with the same love Creator Yahweh has loved us with.

Eagle People...Today's reading is 1 Thessalonians 5:1-11. *Pleya gi.* "Go with Blessings."

December 15

Respect & Honor

W arriors, it is important that we respect those among our people who work hard in serving our Creator Yahweh and who are over us as leaders. Hold them in highest regard because of their work. Let us live in peace with one another and accept admonishment from our leaders (when it comes) as words of wisdom. Let us listen well when they warn of error and kindly exhort us of wrong doing.

Then, in turn, I urge you brothers and sisters, warn those who are idle, encourage the timid, help the weak, be patient with everyone. Make sure that nobody pays back wrong for wrong, but always try to be kind to each other and to everyone else.

We are a family! Let us work diligently to gather provision and share with those in need. Let us encourage one another to fly like eagles above the cares of this world. This is a precious gift we can give...one of respect and honor...first to our Great Chief and Captain and then to one another.

Eagle People...Today's reading is 1 Thessalonians 5:12-15. *Pleya gi.* "Go with Blessings."

December 16

Pray Continually

W arriors, be joyful always! Joy is an act of the heart in response to our Great Chief and Captain. When sorrow falls on us, let us pray.

When worry darkens our path, let us pray. When anxiety clinches our hearts, let us pray! Let us pray continually, lifting our thoughts and even our sighs to Creator Yahweh.

Give thanks in all circumstances, whether good or bad, because you know that our Great Chief and Captain cares for us. He is here with us whether we scale sun drenched forests or crawl through stormy canyons; whether we walk with those who love us or those who side with our enemy, that evil trickster.

Creator Yahweh, the One who calls you, is faithful. He will fill you with Spirit power!

Eagle People…Today's reading is 1 Thessalonians 5:16-18. *Pleya gi.* "Go with Blessings."

December 17

Spirit Fire

Warriors, let us not forget that we are Spirit people! We have always walked with one foot in the spiritual realm. Let us continue to do so. Let it not be said of us that we quench or suppress Holy Spirit power. Let us not put out the Holy Spirit's fire!

Do not our elders still dream dreams? Do not our young people have visions? Let us listen carefully and not despise or scoff at their prophetic revelations, but instead, let us test and prove all things. Let us ask for wisdom from Creator Yahweh until we can recognize what is good and hold fast to it.

Eagle People…Today's reading is 1 Thessalonians 5:19-20. *Pleya gi.* "Go with Blessings."

December 18

Cling to What is Good

Test everything warriors! Avoid every kind of evil. Shrink from it. Stay away from it in whatever form or kind it may appear. Flee from evil situations. Cling to what is good. This is the way of walking in Beauty by approving what is good and lovely and just.

May Creator Yahweh himself, the God of peace, sanctify you through and through. May your whole spirit, soul and body be kept blameless at the coming of our Great Chief and Captain. The One who called you is the same one who paid the price for all your wrong doing. He is faithful. He will keep you blameless.

This is cause for rejoicing warriors! Through Spirit power we are lifted on eagle wings above the circumstances of this world. Keep your eyes on the goal and your feet on the Beauty Way.

Eagle People...Today's reading is 1 Thessalonians 5:21-28. *Pleya gi.* "Go with Blessings."

December 19

Refined Like Silver

Warriors, shout for joy to Creator Yahweh, the creator of all things in heaven and on earth. Sing the glory of his name. Dance before him in glorious praise. How awesome are his deeds! How great is his power. He gave life to all living things. He created us unique and beautiful in his sight.

Look back and see. Remember the things he has done. He has preserved our lives and kept our feet from slipping. He has tested us; and refined us like silver. We have been through fire and water yet he has brought us to a spacious place where we can know him as our Great Chief and Captain.

This is the One we serve. Cry out to him with your whole heart. He will not withhold his great love.

Eagle People...Today's reading is Psalm 66. *Pleya gi.* "Go with Blessings."

December 20

The Great Gathering

Remember warriors that Creator Yahweh, Maker of heaven and earth, our awesome Great Chief and Captain, keeps his covenant of love with those who love him and obey his commands. He does not faint or sleep. His eyes are always open, and his ears ready to listen to the prayers of his servants and warriors as we offer up prayers day and night.

If we are unfaithful to him, refusing to obey his commands and failing to exalt his name, then we bring dishonor to ourselves and our people and he will scatter us among the nations. And rightly so! Because he is our Maker. But if we return to him with our whole hearts and make it our goal to obey his commands, then even if we are exiled to the ends of the hearth, he will gather us beneath his great wings into a dwelling he has chosen.

We are his servants and his chosen people. He has redeemed us by his great strength and saved us with his mighty hand. Some trust in chariots and some trust in horses, but let us trust in the faithfulness of our Creator!

Eagle People...Today's reading is Nehemiah 1.
Pleya gi. "Go with Blessings."

December 21

Rest Well

Warriors, be careful of those who judge you harshly by rules and laws. The law of Creator Yahweh is good if used properly, but it was not made for warriors who walk the Beauty Way. It was made for lawbreakers and rebels, the ungodly and sinful, the unholy and irreligious.

There was a time we walked in those ways, but now that we have given our lives to our Great Chief and Captain we no longer live in rebellion. We have Holy Spirit power to lead us and tell us what is right and wrong! We need no one else to judge us. Our hearts are at rest in the presence of our Great Chief and Captain. Rest well, warriors. This battle has already been won.

Eagle People...Today's reading is 1 Timothy 1:1-13.
Pleya gi. "Go with Blessings."

December 22

Waters of Refreshing

To our Great Chief and Captain, the King Eternal, Immortal, Invisible, the only God, be honor and glory for ever and ever! Let us give thanks to Creator Yahweh who has granted us strength and empowered us to walk the Beauty Way. Yes, there are times we do wrong. Yes, there are times we think wrong thoughts. But Jesus Yeshua has already judged and counted us faithful and trustworthy simply because we have placed our faith in him.

Warriors, we obtain mercy from Creator Yahweh. This is because when we walked the old way of rebellion we did so out of ignorance and unbelief. Now, when we do or think wrongly, Spirit power reminds us to let go of our rebellion. Once we let go of the old way of thinking, the grace of our Great Chief and Captain, and his abundant faith and love flows out on us beyond measure.

Dive into the clean water of Creator Yahweh and be restored and renewed. Let us hold fast to this amazing truth!

Eagle People...Today's reading is 1 Timothy 1:14-17. *Pleya gi.* "Go with Blessings."

December 23

The Great Mystery

In the beginning was Creator Yahweh and Creator Yahweh was with our Great Chief and Captain, and Creator Yahweh was our Great Chief and Captain. He was with our Great Chief and Captain in the beginning. This is a great mystery—that the One who was here, who created all things seen and unseen, can also be born of a human at a specific time and place.

Through Creator Yahweh all things were made; without him nothing was made that has been made. He is the Word spoken that created all things. He is Truth shouting in the streets. He is Wisdom tucked inside our hearts. In him was life, and that life was the Light of all people. The Light shines in the darkness, but the darkness has not understood or grasped it. Yet some have understood and some have received this Light! Receive this Light, warriors, and you will never be the same again. You will soar as on eagle wings, carrying your prayers to the heart of our Great Chief and Captain.

Perhaps you have already received this Light but have hidden it so deep inside that you are no longer aware of the Truth running through your veins. Climb the Sacred Mountain, whether in Spirit or in body, and be still before Creator Yahweh. Listen until His Truth rings loud and clear.

Eagle People...Today's reading is John 1:1-9.
Pleya gi. "Go with Blessings."

December 24

The Word Became Flesh

Creator Yahweh was "...in the world, and though the world was made through him, the world did not recognize him. He came to that which was his own, but his own did not receive him. Yet to all who received him, to those who believed in his name, he gave the right to become children of *our Great Chief and Captain—*children born not of natural descent, nor of human decision or a husband's will, but born of *Creator Yahweh.*

"The Word became flesh and lived for a while among us. We have seen his glory, the glory of the one and only Son, who came from the Father, full of grace and truth." John 1:10-14 (NIV)

These are the ones who proclaim that the Life appeared! The Eternal Life, which was with the Father and has appeared on Earth. When we open our Hearts to Creator Yahweh we have fellowship with one another and the blood of Jesus Yeshua cleanses us from all sins. Creator Yahweh is Light. In him there is no darkness at all.

Eagle People...Today's reading is
John 1:10-14 & 1 John 1:1-5.
Pleya gi. "Go with Blessings."

December 25

Salvation!

Today we take time to celebrate what happened many years ago, in the town of David a Savior has been born to you; he is Christ, Creator Yahweh.

Through him we receive salvation from our enemies and from the hand of all who hate us. This Savior is raised up to show mercy to our fathers, to remember his holy covenant with the ancient ones, and fulfill the oath he swore so long ago. He will rescue us from the hand of our enemies, and enable us to serve him without fear in holiness and righteousness before him all our days. If we let him, he will guide our feet into the path of peace.

This is a call for rejoicing warriors! Raise your voices! Strike the drum! Dance before him with all your might. Do not be afraid. This is good news of great joy that will be for all people. Today is the day of salvation.

Eagle People...Today's reading is Luke 1:67-2:1-14.
Pleya gi. "Go with Blessings."

December 26

Our Youth is Renewed!

Warriors let us give glory to our Great Chief and Captain. Let us praise the Holy name of Creator Yahweh and let us not forget his benefits. He forgives all our wrongdoing and heals our diseases; he redeems our lives from the pit and crowns us with love and compassion; and he satisfies our desires with good things so that our youth is renewed like the eagle's.

Creator Yahweh works righteousness and justice for all the oppressed. Wait for it. It will come and it will not be a day late. Creator Yahweh is compassionate and gracious, slow to anger and abounding in love. He will not always accuse nor will he harbor his anger forever; he does not treat us as our wrongdoing deserves, nor does he repay us according to our evil ways. For as high as the heavens are above the earth, so great is his love for those warriors who fear him. As far as the east is from the west, so far has he removed our guilt from us.

Let us give respect and honor to this ONE above all others. May our lives be poured out in service to our Great Chief and Captain.

Eagle People...Today's reading is Psalm 103:1-12.
Pleya gi. "Go with Blessings."

December 27

Called by Name

Do not be discouraged warriors. As a loving father has compassion on his children, so Creator Yahweh has compassion on those who honor and respect him; for he knows how we are formed. He remembers that we are but dust. Before even one of our days came to be, he knew every mistake we would ever make. Yet he called us by name to be his children forevermore. All we need do is acknowledge him and respond in love.

Our days here on earth are like the grass, like a flower of the field. The wind blows over it and it is gone, and it is remembered no more. Not so with Creator Yahweh! He is from everlasting to everlasting and his love endures forevermore. His righteousness stays with us and with our children's children—with all warriors who keep his covenant and remember to love him and obey his commands. And his commands are simple, warriors, to love him and love others.

If we love Creator Yahweh and love our brothers and sisters, then we will do well and walk in Beauty all the days of our lives here on earth. And then his Spirit will raise us to live with him forevermore.

Eagle People...Today's reading is Psalm 103:13-18. *Pleya gi.* "Go with Blessings."

December 28

Formed in His Image

Do not forget warriors, that Creator Yahweh has established his throne in heaven, and his kingdom rules over all. Even the angels praise his name, the mighty ones who do his bidding and obey his every word. All the heavenly hosts, all the spiritual beings in all worlds, all who honor his commands also praise his holy name.

How can we do less? We who are formed in his image, created by his own hands and who carry his breath of life. Praise Creator Yahweh, O my soul! Our Great Chief and Captain is very great! He is clothed with splendor and majesty. He wraps himself in light as with a garment; he stretches out the heavens like a tent and lays the poles of his upper chambers on their waters. He makes the clouds his chariot and rides on the wings of the wind. He makes winds his messengers, flames of fire his servants.

Listen very carefully, warriors, he may talk with you in a vision, in a dream in the late hours of night. He may whisper in your ear as you climb the Sacred Mountain. His words my clench your soul as your read the *Sacred Writings.* Give ear to his words, heed his commands, and find life and rest for your weary soul.

Eagle People...Today's reading is
Psalm 103:19-104:1-4.
Pleya gi. "Go with Blessings."

December 29

Satisfied with Good Things

Have you ever considered, warriors, how the trees of Creator Yahweh are well watered? The birds of the air do not reap or sow, yet our Great Chief and Captain feeds them. The moon marks off the seasons, and the sun knows when to sleep. How many are the works of Creator Yahweh! In wisdom he made all that has been made. The earth is full of his creatures, both great and small. There is the sea, vast and spacious, teeming with creatures beyond number. There the ships go to and fro, and the leviathan, that great animal our eyes have never seen, frolics upon the great waters.

These all look to Creator Yahweh to give them their food at the proper time. Should we not do the same? He gives us food and we gather it up; when he opens his hand we are satisfied with good things. Yet when he hides his face, we are terrified, and when he takes our breath away we die and return to the dust.

Do not fear warriors, for dust is not the end of our people. Jesus Yeshua has conquered sin by giving his life for us and he has conquered death by rising from the dead. In so doing, he released Spirit power that will restore our bodies and renew the face of the earth. This is the promise given to all warriors who have chosen to walk The Jesus Way. Stand firm, brothers and sisters, your faith will not be in vain.

Eagle People ... Today's reading is Psalm 104:5-30.
Pleya gi. "Go with Blessings."

December 30

Dance before Him

Let us sing to Creator Yahweh all the days of our lives! May our feet dance before him as long as strength remains. May the thoughts we think day in and day out be pleasing to our Great Chief and Captain. Give thanks to Creator Yahweh, call upon his name. Make known among the nations what he has done. He has chosen us to be his people. He has called us each by name. He has remembered his covenant forever. Let us give glory to his holy name.

Look to Creator Yahweh and his strength. Do not trust in the strength of humans. Seek the face of Creator Yahweh above all beauty the world has to offer. Remember the wonders he has done, the miracles and the judgments he pronounced.

He promised a Savior and became one himself. He promised restoration and made that possible through the cross. He promised resurrection and set the example. Our wounds will be healed and our hearts restored. Strength will return to our weary bones. Shouts of joy will once again be heard in the camp! Do not become weary in well doing, warriors, for at just the right time, we will reap a harvest, and it will not be a day late.

Eagle People...Today's reading is Psalm 104:31-105:5.
Pleya gi. "Go with Blessings."

December 31

Arrayed in Majesty

Listen, warriors, Creator Yahweh is at your right hand. He will crush kings on the day of his wrath. He will judge the nations, heaping up the dead and crushing the rulers of the whole earth. Your troops will be willing on your day of battle. Arrayed in holy majesty, from the womb of the dawn, you will receive the dew of your youth.

Our Great Chief and Captain has sworn these promises and he will not change his mind. His promises are sure and true. He stands at the right hand of the needy ones to save their lives from those who condemn them. Cry out to Creator Yahweh in your trouble, he will save you from your distress. He will bring you out of darkness and the deepest gloom and break away your chains. Give thanks to our Great Chief and Captain for his unfailing love and his wonderful deeds for men, for he breaks down gates of bronze and cuts through bars of iron.

Eagle People...Today's reading is
Psalm 107:10-16 & 43 & Psalm 110.
Pleya gi. "Go with Blessings."

ABOUT THE AUTHORS

GHOSTDANCER SHADLEY (Also known as Cal, Buttons and Pahowatush) was a respected elder of the Klamath and Warm Springs tribes of Oregon. It was his desire to leave a legacy of doing the will of God with a focus on reaching out to others with God's love. He succeeded in that during his lifetime, and now his ministry continues through the written word.

SANDY CATHCART is a freelance writer, photographer and artist, as well as a scribe for Restoring The Heart Ministries. She lives in the High Cascades of Southern Oregon with her husband, The Cat Man, where she writes about Creator and everything wild.

www.ingramcontent.com/pod-product-compliance
Lightning Source LLC
Chambersburg PA
CBHW031544040426
42452CB00006B/182